A Jour[...] of Life On
Purpose

Creativity, Love, Womanhood,
Community, Race, and Identity

Nonfiction

AVRIL SOMERVILLE

www.somerempress.com
SomerEmpress Publishing

Published in the United States by SomerEmpress Publishing.

ISBN-10: 9-9621690l
ISBN-13: 978-0996216906

FIRST EDITION

DEDICATION

A Journey Of Life On Purpose: Creativity, Love, Womanhood, Community, Race, and Identity is dedicated to my late grandmother and first woman mother faith influence, Susan Vernice Johnson Nibbs.

It is written for all who seek to share their gifts with the world. For them, no gift is too small, no time is too little, and no space insignificant.

Where my feet will take me, I will go
When my heart is open, I can only grow
Even the best-laid plans have detours
Twists and turns
But I'll arrive ... still ... heart intact
Open to love
Open to receive
Beyond anything my heart can ever conceive
I arrive, heart intact, open to love, open to receive

—AVRIL SOMERVILLE,
Onward

CONTENTS

YEARNING: ONCE A MOTHER, TWICE A CHILD

PURPOSEFUL INTENTIONS

HARNESSING THE CREATIVE SPIRIT

Acknowledgments

I thank God for the divine inspirations and revelations that brought this book to Life. I am thankful for my wonderful husband Rodney, whose incredible support and constancy of love during the entire preparation of this book made it that more urgent and possible. I am thankful for the daily inspiration and delight of our three children who restore the simplicity of living to what we adults often make complex.

I give thanks for mi hermana and dear editor Loretta "FunkyLB" Brown, who held me to an uncompromising standard of quality and craftsmanship during the entire process. The women readers who gathered with us as we moved closer to completion were remarkably candid and razor-sharp as they made capable recommendations for streamlining the overall focus and arc of this book. Lastly, I am thankful for my extended network of woman prayer warrior friends, who revel in the brilliance of our collective light.

Prologue

You could have picked up any book, but you picked up *A Journey Of Life On Purpose: Creativity, Love, Womanhood, Community, Race, and Identity*. Something drew you in on this day, so you are not here by default, but by design. Call it Spirit, God, whatever you will, but in some way or another, there is an alignment and urgency that led you here. This conviction is also the same impetus for the writing of this book. Life does not happen to us, but rather, because of us; as such, we are capable of co-designing and shaping our own lives. Through application of the epiphanies revealed to us in our quiet time when we are most attentive to Spirit, we have the ability to be creative life artists and willing sculptors.

You might be at a stage of your life where life's richness and fullness escapes you. This is possibly due to routine, necessity and sameness of work, tending to everyone else's spirit but yours, or some combination of these reasons. You know there is more to life, but the potential for real meaning is fleeting because of life's hurried pace. The preponderance of social media, technology, and the warp-speed delivery of bad news and all things sensational make it even more difficult to find meaning. You want more, and reach for more, yet the design part of life feels elusive, something that you very well may never achieve. Though you intuitively believe that something special resides within you, you find yourself in need of a little motivation and introspection to extract it, to get beyond simply believing, and to live for real.

Life is like a river, constant and unyielding. As rivers course through tributaries, through and around obstacles, they feed and sustain, effortlessly providing life to all they encounter. Some rivers rage, while others are calm, yet they all seem to have a quiet certainty about them. Rivers refresh and replenish without our asking; life has this same ability, but unlike the river, we have to fuel life. Just as the river prepares the ground for fertility, life prepares and shapes us for breakthroughs and further grounding, but first we must show up as active agents.

A Journey Of Life On Purpose is a declaration that life already has an inherent energy, set into motion many moons ago–long before we got here, and in order to benefit from the fullness of this energy, we must also unapologetically bring a compatible energy in order to experience ultimate authenticity and self-actualization. The resultant synergy that comes from the alignment of these two energies–life's and our own–compels us to live life as if we were artists commissioned to create our biggest masterpiece yet, deliberately and purposefully, with intention and design. Written to motivate introspection, and engage the silent confirmations felt in our most everyday experiences, this book is an invitation to journey with me along the river of life, one whose origins and destinations are unknown, but one that we know flows constantly, awakening life's energy wherever its current may lead. This invitation to "get in the flow" requires that you first show up; second, bring your best energy; and lastly, be attentive to life as it unfolds, one experience and one encounter at a time. The journey can only be made more dynamic based on what you bring with you or leave behind.

It is my hope that the convictions collected from my own journey along life's river, delivered through personal essays and poetry, resonate and affirm you in the way that a hug from a loving grandmother can, graciously and lovingly. If she hugs too hard, it might be uncomfortable, but you know that she does so in the spirit of love. While the experiences are personal, I do not come alone, but rather, I am connected to a larger web of persons—ancestors, poets, songwriters, elder women of wit and wisdom, ministers, prayer warriors, survivors, mothers, caretakers, wives, daughters, healers, and life seekers—with whom some of these truths and experiences are also shared.

The selections are independent of each other, but together they represent insight gained from stillness on matters such as love, transparency, sisterhood, empathy, intentionality, community, race, creativity, purpose, marriage, child rearing, spirituality, and self-actualization. At the time of writing, they felt urgent, like the urging of some creative spirit to record them; therefore, I believe that they will also reframe the urgency of life and purpose in someone else upon reading. These contemplations are authenticated by an experiential knowledge that can only be gained from the intersection of experiences as a Black woman wife mother daughter friend artist spirit servant immigrant.

For The Love Of Us

Love shoves despair and destitution
back into their respective corners,
Confirms and accepts the deciduousness of our blues.
Love knows, wants to know.
Forces us to ask and contend with our most gut wrenching
and troubling questions,
Grows us ... somehow.

—AVRIL SOMERVILLE,
Love Unmasked

The River Flows

I can still hear the verses of the gospel hymn, "Shall We Gather at the River?" written by Robert Lowry, play over in my mind. The song continued long after I stopped living with my grandmother, and even after she made her physical transition from this earth. Whether she sang aloud in my presence as a child while she cooked, washed, cleaned, or sewed, I could recognize the song by her humming alone.

The hymn began with an invitation to gather at the river. Regardless of your belief or unbelief, the journey along a river is apparently one worth taking. The river in this text is a communal space full of life and potential, where ancestors and loved ones still inspire and speak to and through us; it is that metaphysical place where those still living go for hope, seeking a "crystal" and "flowing tide" that replenishes the soul through Spirit.

> *Yes, we'll gather at the river,*
> *The beautiful, the beautiful river;*
> *Gather with the saints at the river*
> *That flows by the throne of God.*

The above refrain answers and affirms that yes, we will gather together at the river. In that act alone, we acknowledge that, in our gathering, we each need something from a source more divine, and beyond ourselves alone. We agree that it is a "beautiful" place regardless of our belief. We are aligned in one belief that the river is indeed a source from a greater power, Spirit, and perhaps even God. In our agreement, we defy tradition by declaring the spiritual authority within us, and are of the position that in our gathering, there is undisputed power and sustenance that we can obtain from such a beautiful and necessary place.

On the margin of the river,
Washing up its silver spray,
We will walk and worship ever,
All the happy golden day.

The refrain continues to declare both the powerful beauty and beautiful power of the river. Even "on the margin," a place where many of us often find ourselves, whether because of a systematic oppression of some kind, or because of some more personal and deep-seated impoverishment—we are still capable of achieving community. Despite circumstance, we neither lose our praise nor surrender to the whims of the winds around us, but rather, we actively participate in our life's unfolding. We don't sit idly by the river, or simply stand on its sidelines in bewilderment, but rather, engage in the life produced and sustained by the river. We walk—both on the frontlines and within the margins—toward a central energy that draws us in with a power of hope so strong that we can't help but be joyful and rejoice that something mystical, powerful, and beautiful is brewing in each of us as well as underfoot, even as we walk.

Ere we reach the shining river,
Lay we every burden down;
Grace our spirits will deliver,
And provide a robe and crown.

"Ere"—that is, before—we reach that river, we must commit to being undaunted by its uneven tide, choppy waters, or potential depth. We must work in earnest to release our personal baggage and shed our fears. We cannot possibly come to the river, expecting to retrieve refreshment if we are weighted down with stuff—physical, material, or otherwise.

In our reflections, seen only through the "shining," gleaming surface of the river, we will be able to see, embrace, and ultimately activate our inherent power. But first, we will need to pick up our courage and lay our burdens down. We must relieve ourselves of the weights that have held us captive for so long, threatening to extinguish the very life, promises and purposes borne in us long ago. Only then will our spirits graciously yield to something far more lasting than a robe and a crown, but rather, to personal fulfillment and purpose in our journey, regardless of the fires we've had to endure or the bridges we've had to cross to get there.

> *Soon we'll reach the shining river,*
> *Soon our pilgrimage will cease;*
> *Soon our happy hearts will quiver*
> *With the melody of peace.*

This last verse moves us further toward our reward. Our arrival at the river suggests the possibility for peace, and marks a celebratory unveiling and unlocking of a peace that can only begin here. The dissonance of a life marked by strife, insecurities, worry, anxiety, and fear takes its rightful place—in our unforgiving pasts, before we knew our strength—and is replaced by a formidable clarity that the journey was well worth it!

Our hearts "quiver" as we feel ourselves align with our inherent power that till now had been unknown, untrusted, and unacknowledged. At the river, we are replenished, washed anew, and strengthened. There, we become part of something greater. We no longer stand alone, but commune one with another in the collective spirit that is needed to propel us forward, both together and alone. We emerge, each of us, stronger than when we first came—intact, resilient yet vulnerable, whole though broken, loved, full, forgiven, and most certainly capable.

The River is Life, and it flows in all that we do. Shall we gather?

FOR THE LOVE OF US

Don't Talk to Strangers

The more I write, the more aware and appreciative I become of my own voice and the less need I have for validation from others. I do have some wonderfully supportive people in my corner—friends and family—with whom I communicate on a regular basis. Still, there are others that I've never seen in person who play as much a role in inspiring me and holding me accountable to my gifts.

Through social media, we can share our convictions and interests—heart matters—with people from diverse walks of life who we might not actually know. This isn't to say that everyone who uses social media uses it positively toward this end. Also, connections made via social media are not entirely random; there is usually a connection or unifier. In some cases, the connection is a mutual friend, cause, or place; in yet other instances, it is what I call an *orchestration by Spirit* of like-minded souls. In turn, we draw energy from an alignment that feels purposeful.

In this space we feel that we have a tabula rasa—a cleaner slate—a chance to begin anew, with the possibility of making newer connections that don't judge as quickly or harshly. By all appearances, there are no true expectations of these connections; should we shut them off, we can continue with our lives just as we did before making them. One thing that intrigues me most about this space is the heightened potential for empathy. Rather than interpreting what a person shares through the lens of their history or an ulterior motive, we tend to focus instead, more objectively, on the singularity of what is shared for its rightfulness or wrongness, and sometimes simply for its practicality or usefulness.

I think, too, that the ease with which more personal

information is shared on social media is somewhat akin to the guy at the bar who feels more comfortable opening up to a bartender about his personal affairs, but not to fellow parishioners at a church, because he knows unequivocally that he will be judged. Perhaps he is also judged at the bar, but with a lowered guard and a newfound inebriety, he worries about little beyond that moment of sharing. Plus, he's partly paying for someone else to listen to him, so no one cares whether he talks all night.

Just like the man at the bar, all we might be getting in these online exchanges with strangers is a listening ear or watchful reader—a mere fraction of what we *think* we're missing from our real-life relationships. Unlike the man at the bar, we must approach our online encounters with a level of discernment and caution. Everyone does not have our best interest at heart, and people *will* judge.

Social media has its limits as well as its lessons. Surely, if we can support those we know nothing about personally, we can do a better job of supporting those we *do* know in our real life——the ones we claim to love, the dysfunctional family that we can't exchange for another, the real-life people with whom we have to interact on a most regular basis. We should also be a blessing to these folk, and lift them up as they move ahead in their respective life journeys regardless of where we are in our own. We should also celebrate them when their dreams are materialized and reserve our need to judge. We are as capable of extending that same kindness to them, as they are of receiving it.

Perhaps we can call them directly from time to time or write them a personal line or two of encouragement. We can promote their work or simply share in the excitement that they can't seem to keep to themselves. Maybe we can commit to memory one of the dreams they've confided in us and encourage them in this regard. For me, it helps to jot a few notes when having a phone conversation with someone I haven't spoken with in a while; this way, I am more likely to follow up on what is important to them in subsequent discussions. Connecting in more meaningful ways with people we claim to know and love over time, will be a cornerstone of our authenticity and self-growth, versus those relationships that will only come and go.

A Recipe for Love

What is love? Being married alone doesn't suggest love. You can't experience love from a partner until you first find and create love. Relying on your partner to be your sole source of love is a burden too heavy for even the most patient and understanding person to bear. Eventually, the pressure of the weight will snap love's branches. You cannot expect to love someone fully or be fully loved by someone until you have first nurtured a love of self, a love in honoring or doing something that is greater than yourself, or an intrinsic happiness and Joy that comes from fulfilling a purpose or passion that no relationship alone can provide. When you're grounded in something that is larger and more meaningful, you agonize less about love and romance, become less anxious, and in turn, facilitate love's entry.

Love is not a singular act, but rather a process, an undertaking. Perhaps this is why the act of marriage is accompanied by a contract that bears the names and consent of both parties. Marriage is truly a labor of love.

Too often, I witness couples that have been married for several years, yet their love seems lackluster at best. They show up at public functions together, but seem so far apart emotionally. There is no holding of hands, no touching, no exchanging of blushing smiles, and no display of other outward affection or intimacy between the two. They seem to have accepted this stage of their marriage as if somehow this is what marriage is supposed to devolve into—a quiet given tucked away somewhere, where love no longer needs to be cultivated. The fire died a long time ago because they stopped kindling and tending to the flame.

By my own admission, I've sometimes made it hard for my husband to love me. I had so many restrictions. Part of it had to do with the difficulty of me being able to make the switch from the mommy of our children to being my husband's wife and lover. Women wear many hats, and our ability to tend to multiple things at once sometimes leaves us feeling less than "in the mood." As a result, our partners might find themselves having to expend a disproportionate amount of energy when it comes to romance.

The love/hate relationship I had with my body also made it difficult to avail myself to love. I was so busy being my own worst critic that my husband's flattery and attempts to love me went undetected, much less reciprocated. All I could see were my physical flaws and shortcomings. I may as well have been wearing a sign that read "Off Duty" or "Do Not Enter," when all I was trying to convey was "bear with me, I am still 'Under Construction.'" Imagine what that must feel like to the person who already sees you as perfect.

In order to enjoy making love, we first have to nurture a love for ourselves by rejecting preconceived notions of youth and bodily perfection. Embracing that we are perfectly imperfect and made like no one else should affirm that we are perfect enough and worthy of love. Only then, can we be available to love; only then can love bloom.

Also, love requires our flexibility and a receptiveness to love not just on our terms, but on our partner's as well. We have to resist the urge to be a command and control center for the act of love and learn to be more patient with our partners. Believe it or not, they're still learning to love us. There is a thin line between telling your lover what you like, and shooting them down for their attempts to love us, as only they know how. Special requests and adjustments should be recommended in the spirit of love, and not with criticism that only leaves your lover feeling defeated or undesirable, and you feeling badly for asking.

Co-write your recipe for love so that what you end up with is truly remarkable—personalized and pleasurable—perfectly suited for just the two of you. Create your own fireworks as you engage in the explosiveness of love! Don't become like the couple that no longer delights in holding hands or kissing each other. Kindle the flames; keep the fire hot!

For Just the Two of Us

At the recommendation of a dear friend, I sat to watch the film documentary *Still Bill*, featuring the great singer and songwriter Bill Withers. Mr. Withers had not yet been inducted into the Rock and Roll Hall of Fame at the production of this documentary. I knew the film would be first-rate because my friend is not only a music connoisseur, but is also an incredibly talented musician. She knows great music and appreciates a good story. I was already familiar with Bill's more popular songs, including "Ain't No Sunshine," and "Grandma's Hands," though not with Bill, the man. As I watched, I very quickly grew captivated by the story of Bill's upbringing, how he fell into music, and how music found him. I became engrossed in his musings on life's nuances and instructions, as well as his own vulnerabilities and transparent introspection.

I learned of Bill's love of family—his wife, and son and daughter—and his insistence on simple living. I remain intrigued by, but deeply understand, his walking away from the music industry when he could no longer create on his own terms; choosing instead to be more hands-on as a husband and parent, while still writing music, sometimes with his daughter Kori, also a singer and songwriter. I found Bill beautifully human and whole, as he reflected on both his childhood and his contentious battle with the music industry, and with life in general.

As one who overcame chronic stuttering, Bill placed a premium on the solace that he found writing songs. He recollected with fondness, the stern and steady rhythm of his grandmother, a woman who perhaps had the most profound impact on shaping his perspectives about life and love. No doubt, she was the inspiration for his song "Grandma's Hands." I was delighted to meet Bill, the man behind the music, who sang about what sounded like a rare and coveted love in "Just the Two of Us."

I recalled my own first impressions upon hearing "Just the Two of Us" as a young girl living in the West Indies on the island of Antigua. Of course, I knew nothing about that kind of love then, but it sure sounded beautiful! As an adult, before I found love and love found me, I would get all dreamy-eyed as I fantasized about one day having a love like the one Withers described. Naturally, I was filled with nostalgia when I again heard the words:

> *I see the crystal raindrops fall*
> *And the beauty of it all*
> *Is when the sun comes shining through*
> *To make those rainbows in my mind*
> *When I think of you sometime*
> *And I want to spend some time with you*

As I became even more absorbed in Bill's story, and listened to the words over the narrator's voice, I asked myself whether this special kind of love, so aptly and poetically penned over thirty years ago, really exists. I looked over at my husband, just then, on the sofa, and felt something magical, even from where I sat. I was having a full-circle moment to my giddy nine-year old self who wondered what that kind of love was all about when she first heard the song.

> *Just the two of us*
> *Building castles in the sky*
> *Just the two of us*
> *You and I*

I was experiencing the just-the-two-of-us kind of love that I fantasized about as a young girl! It *was* just the two of us, sometimes against the world, navigating life's sea of changes and our personal challenges, yet we managed to still be beautifully in love. Our eyes met and affirmed what I already felt inside: our connection needed no words. We were quietly reflecting on the gift that life had given us … love itself. This verse of Withers' classic sums it up perfectly.

> *We look for love, no time for tears*
> *Wasted waters' all that is*
> *And it don't make no flowers grow*
>
> *Good things might come to those who wait*
> *Not to those who wait too late*
> *We got to go for all we know.*

FOR THE LOVE OF US

What Really Matters

Learning of the death of my friend's husband jarred me to my core. My friend was only an acquaintance at the time, but I knew that it wouldn't be long before we became closer given how I felt upon hearing the devastating news of her husband's passing. He was no older than my husband. In addition to his wife, his two children, both of whom were close to my own children in age, survived him.

Though our lives did not intersect as they did with closer friends and family, it was difficult to go through the routines of my day without thinking about them. As I prepared my children for the morning, made breakfast, and called up to my husband that coffee was ready, I was mindful of the small, yet significant ways that loved ones tend to each other. I became keenly aware of the importance of nurture and not just responsibility; the role of a steady and comforting hand beyond duty, that encourages and consoles, and reminds us of the worth of our physical presence and the invaluable ways in which we make life easier and more meaningful for each other.

On this bitterly cold and snowy day, my husband woke up to plow and line the driveway and sidewalk with salt, and warm up my car.

"Just in case you need to run out with the kids, baby," he cried out.

I thanked him kindly, although I had no intention of driving in such weather. He was swift in his movements and deliberate in the use of his time, as he would soon need to leave for work. Work never ends for him and the office never seems to be closed. Whether he feels like it or not, he reports to work so he can better care and provide for us because one of the ways he measures success is by his ability to do so. I am aware of the weight of this, though he has never once complained that it is a burden. He takes great pride in what he does, and how he does it, and expresses gratitude at every turn for the work that I also do for our family at home, which doesn't fit neatly into a "job," per se.

I would often remark that he doesn't get it—the entanglement of all that I do to keep our household running smoothly while being on call around-the-clock for our children and him—however, I believe that he does get it on the most important levels. In that sense, there is indeed balance and harmony. In the most intimate sense, there is a flow that allows for a quiet understanding of the choices we've made for our family, how they affect our present circumstances, and the sacrifices that they will continue to require of us.

Still, on that snowy day, I didn't think about our shortcomings or sacrifices, or about him not getting it; but rather, about my new friend, and what she would do just for the physical presence of her husband. I considered the myriad of everyday matters and gaps in which she would now need others to stand where her husband stood so dutifully. My faith informs me to care for widows and orphans, and that I will, but my personal compass, guided by that same faith, convicts me that there is yet a multitude of ways that we need to be more present for the ones we love.

At the end of the day, the only audience that will matter is the one that consists of our loved ones, not Facebook friends or Twitter followers, or the host of others—employers, coworkers, professional and organizational affiliations—in which we already invest too much of our precious time. They, too, have lives that need tending and should prioritize doing so; they must learn to manage in our absence.

Before we can give anyone and anything else yet another day, let us first tend to those who matter and to the urgent matters of our heart—the ones that will outlast long after our computers and handhelds go up in smoke, long after we have lost loved ones, long after our employers replace us, and certainly long after our children have gone on and made lives of their own. Tend to those heart matters while you can, because if you blink too long, you just might miss it! Everyone and everything else can wait.

My Sister, My Self

Like a peacock that knows her beauty,
An inner dance, an outward flamboyance.
Each plume exacted,
Purposeful,
Beheld.

—AVRIL SOMERVILLE,
The Stare-Down

Writing to Heal

I completed the first draft of my first novel by writing every single day one November as part of the National Novel Writing Month (NaNoWriMo) challenge. This made me an official NaNoWriMo winner for finishing a novel of at least 50,000 words in thirty days. More than the writing itself, I learned many lessons in the process.

The biggest takeaway was the obvious time commitment that accomplishing this goal entailed. I had to disconnect from social media, and eliminate activities that could otherwise absorb downtime that could be used for writing. I had to slow my cheering for President Barack Obama during his second campaign and unglue myself from the media outtakes of Mitt Romney's ascension and eventual fall from the national spotlight. My main focus needed to be on writing, and I needed the part of my brain responsible for literary abandon and creative thinking to be completely available.

I wanted to keep myself honest and hold myself accountable. I failed the previous year during my first attempt to complete the same challenge, but this time I had a renewed sense of urgency and purpose to write in earnest every day. I had a story to tell and so I began. Nothing would keep me from it this time.

Writing every day was a trying, electrifying, harrowing, sleep-deprived, crazy time. Surprisingly, working this intently toward my novel gave me a personal sense of validation that I didn't know I needed. Participating made me feel that my story was not only important, but also worth telling. In solidarity with other writers, I felt incredibly empowered to take liberties in crafting the story and gave myself permission to misbehave a bit.

Focusing on my novel in this thirty-day window required discipline and a removal of filters. I could not divorce myself from the travails of my characters. As I wrote, I found my characters dealing with deep-seated emotions. Repeatedly, I questioned how their raw emotions engulfed their personas. They didn't gloss over how they felt, whom they betrayed, or even who they did or didn't love. At first, I needed to cleanse them for presentation by glossing over their flaws with masks to hide their deeper, darker dimensions. This was necessary for me to present them in a way that made them digestible, but it was unclear for whom. Stripping their ghosts from their hideous pasts only made them palpable for me to digest, but created a conundrum that I could not reconcile.

For example, what do you do when the wolf who violently attacks Little Red Riding Hood is your brother or father? Do you make excuses for him, love him anyhow, or blame Little Red Riding Hood, the victim, for her shortened skirt, hijab, or flirting smile? Do you confront the wolf with disgust or continue to romanticize his lies? I found myself eager to find a redeeming quality in an otherwise dark character that I didn't like very much.

It became difficult to disconnect from the novel after addressing the layers, plots, and complexities of the characters. This was painful at times, convicting at others, and almost always consuming. I was physically present, but the story kept me awake at night, sabotaged my sleep, and waywardly inserted itself into my daily life with a nagging unpleasantness.

Writing and crafting the story was one of undeniable paradoxes and questions. Could I be liberated from the bullshit and guilt of unfulfilled expectations still nestled deep inside me, or did I need to be positively neutral in all things? Could I call a spade a spade, or should I instead sterilize the characters of flaws, real or imagined? Could I be unapologetically raw and truthful in presenting my characters despite flaws and still keep them whole? Could I, as a writer, not offend anyone who might identify with the characters, and why should I care?

Writing the novel forced me to ascribe a fuller humanity to characters and delve into the dark without censor. It was in unleashing their fullness that the true story would ultimately develop. Inherently, I knew that cleansed and contrived characters could not sustain a novel. I also knew that not all stories end happily ever after. We're all familiar with broken marriages after storybook weddings. This is the same with writing and life in general. Not all stories will fit into neatly packaged presentations, no matter how you craft them.

The lesson in all of this was that writing is full of epiphanies and surprises. You feel liberated when you get the story right, when you feel that you have done justice to the characters, but writing is downright daunting when you have nothing to write at all. Still, you write anyway! You may stop, but do start again until you reach The End ... wherever that may be.

MY SISTER, MY SELF

My Tapestry of Women

One of my biggest inspirations has been the collective and dynamic strength, power, and radiance that I found in the tapestry of women that made my 40th birthday anything but ordinary. The celebration and exchanges made it a "Sweet Summer Indulgence," indeed! For almost half a year, whenever I would think about how I would celebrate my 40th birthday, I would hear the word "authenticity" quietly whispering back to me. "Whatever you do," the voice said, "do it as authentically as only you can."

You will never hear me say, "40 is the new 30." Though the spirit of the saying is appreciated—in that 40 is youthful, radiant, and all those wonderful things—I owe much of my growth and development to the wisdom gained in those additional years. So, I'll still call it 40, and you can keep the change. Forty is what it is: sexy, confident, unapologetic, uncompromising, and can-stand-on-its-own-two-feet. Period. The ferocity and flamboyance that comes with that extra decade is what I longed to don and parade for so long as a young woman, and the occasion of my 40th birthday party provided the perfect opportunity to celebrate with those women who helped to shape me in countless ways.

I decided to invite women to my 40th birthday celebration who either influence or inspire me on a personal level. These were Sistah-friends and comrades, even some who I knew could not attend. But mostly, these were the women who make up a tapestry of genuine womanhood that I know to be special. I wanted to shower them with gratitude, indulge them with love, and honor them as I embarked on this part of my life journey.

First in my tapestry was my mother, the woman who ushered my twin sister and me into this world in what I am sure was a messy birth. Like the edges of a handcrafted afghan, her role was critical in framing my tapestry's coming together on my special day. From margins unseen, she spared me from the potential embarrassment of a less-than-ready-for-guests bathroom. She dug, filled, and beautified otherwise empty flowerbeds with her own wonderful selection of flowers and plants—something that I was not yet physically capable of doing at the time. She waited patiently and attended to my rowdy children while we shopped for birthday outfits that I would have never thought she would have chosen. All I could say was "Wow, go Mom!" Her only goal was to make sure that I presented myself well. She did the things that no one thought of or cared about, but in their absence, would have showed the imperfections that I tried so hard to hide on this occasion. While I got a chance to collect the compliments, it was she who worked quietly behind the scenes to ensure that my celebration went off without a hitch. She made my tapestry come alive.

The word 'beautiful' does not adequately capture how I felt seeing each of my friends in their elegance and gracefulness. As I spent time with each of them individually, I reflected on the occasion of our first encounters. While I knew they were there to celebrate me, I was overwhelmed by the gift of their presence. They were cohesive and independent, yet there was nothing off-putting about them as we danced, laughed, and shared just long enough to create a memory. Their presence made me feel joyful, blessed, and courageous, exactly how I wanted to feel on my birthday! In my celebration with the women who gathered, I realized that it was okay to be included as part of the tapestry and not independent of it as an outsider or standing admirer in an art museum.

By my own admission, I did not always have a tapestry of women in my life, nor did I regard relationships among women from this collective perspective. There's been betrayal from unlikely sources, hurt, unreasonable expectations, misunderstandings, and rejection, which made my tapestry somewhat lacking and uneventful, a far cry from anything as striking or elaborate as a tapestry. It takes a lot of inner work to be a complement to others, without the need for personal attention. To my surprise, I could still thrive as an individual freethinker and still be in community with other incredibly talented women such as those gathered that day. Furthermore, these women have their own tapestry, separate from mine, which I must also celebrate and honor. Somehow, within their tapestry and mine, we can and do reveal a bond that is even more beautiful because of our connectedness.

Unlike a quilt, there are no visibly discernible parts that stand alone in a tapestry. Tapestries are complex, layered, and interwoven; they look best when their intricacy and oneness are displayed, right side up, and not displayed with all the nips and tucks on the backside which hide loose threads and character flaws. In the presentation of the intersection of all of the parts that come to make the tapestry what it is, there are no expectations, and certainly no judgment, because everyone knows how much work was required in its making. Each element of the tapestry represents our strongest desires to express our own uniqueness; yet, because our intersections are so much more elaborate than our individual threads, we understand that we are not to make ourselves look better at the expense of another woman. This tapestry then occupies a space that is sacred where women can simply be; a space where they can experience an outpouring of love that is both necessary and truthful, a space that we clearly deserve and want. It is a space where love transcends our own perceived limitations.

Author, poet, and playwright Dr. Maya Angelou captured the sentiment best when she said, "I've learned that people will forget what you said, forget what you did, but people will never forget how you made them feel." I will never forget how being in fellowship with the women in my tapestry on this special day made me feel.

MY SISTER, MY SELF

Keeping It Real

One night, shortly before retiring to bed, I received a call from a dear friend, with whom I hadn't spoken in almost half a year. As her name flashed across the screen of my cell phone, I adjusted myself on the bed, propping myself up against two pillows, making sure to get real comfortable for what I knew would be a long conversation. Our conversations are always long, but this time, after the first few words and the measured silences in between, I knew that this wouldn't be just one of our ordinary chats. There wasn't going to be any "Girl, let me tell you" this or that, at least not yet. She had something to say that required more than a casual response or perfunctory comment, and she was going to make sure that I listened.

She told me that after much prayer and reflection, she thought that it would be a good time to share with me why she felt that our friendship had changed, and why we hadn't spoken as often. "You mean there's a reason beyond our lives just being full? Who knew?" I thought. I was more than taken off-guard. She shared with me that she had been harboring feelings of anger and resentment toward me for my not being more available for her during the two most difficult periods in her life. Truly, I was taken by surprise because so much time had transpired since those events. Obviously, these feelings had been brewing for a while. Unbeknownst to me, there was no opportunity for me to acknowledge, let alone address them. Rather than dwelling on that, I listened to her very intently, and thought, how big of her it was to even share this with me, after all these years. She had no way of knowing what my reaction would be—denial, rejection, defensiveness—yet she thought enough of our relationship to call and open up to me in this way.

I strongly believe that our emotions are personal, so who am I to contest them? If you say you felt cheated upon, betrayed or otherwise, those are your feelings and you're entitled to them. Nothing I say or do is going to change that. Often however, I believe that we make assumptions about one's intent. It was never my intention to be dismissive or unaffected, but there were legitimate events in my own life that contributed to my absence, or what may have appeared as disengagement. My immersion into my life transitions very well could have clouded my judgment, and obscured my perception of anything outside my nucleus of activity. Throw in being newly married, starting a family, and relocating into the mix. I could clearly see and appreciate her perspective.

But this wasn't about me. This was about my friend's truth, and her need to convey deep-seated feelings that she'd been harboring until then. I was fully open and receptive to letting her tell it, apologized readily, and accepted full responsibility for how hurtful my behavior might have been. This time, I was less interested in "explaining away" a defense and more interested in resuming the relationship. I reveled in the unfolding because I knew that we couldn't move forward as true friends without this moment. Somewhere during our conversation, I had a series of epiphanies; one was that of gratitude—how blessed and thankful I should be for friends who think enough of our friendship to address uncomfortable truths; and the other, that authentic relationship can only come from the unveiling of our most troubling anxieties and even our shortcomings.

Despite my exhaustion that evening, I made it a point to be fully engaged in conversation, and hung on to every word. I cherished the richness of our dialogue as we shared memories and committed to the unbreakable sisterhood that had always characterized our relationship. Needless to say, we talked well into the night, for almost an hour and a half! Not only did we catch up, we left each other feeling lighter, yet remarkably whole.

Diamonds on the Inside

The hunger that constantly aches the soul for a new item, fanfare, or recognition comes from the unattended and underserved places within us. They echo of a hollowness that has been besieged by savvy marketing and products to "cure all," thereby eliminating the need for personal introspection. That same hunger informs an inclination to feed our need rather than feed our spirit. In turn, we attempt to fill that "need" with activities and behavior such as shopping and spending, thereby robbing ourselves of the lasting gifts that can only come from the deep inner work that we can only put off for so long. Our acquisition of stuff and our preoccupation with busyness makes us look and feel good, though only for a short time.

This pattern of behavior is especially pronounced in November and December. Many of us scurry around despite the crowds and inclement weather, in search of presents for loved ones and new items for ourselves, just for the holidays. Whether we do this as ritual, or because there is a sincere impetus in us that makes us feel more generous or grateful during this time of the year remains unknown. Whatever the motivation, one thing most of us will agree on, is that we are probably doing too much. I'd venture to say that some families put more effort into their search for the best deals in hopes of purchasing every last item on their Christmas list, before they give thanks at Thanksgiving, if that is even a part of their tradition. On one hand, they maintain that they are thankful, yet they are not content.

Despite the acquisition of more, many of us remain largely unsatisfied. Though we know it won't be long before we will be inhabited by that same emptiness after the novelty of a new item wears off, we continue to overdo. We attempt to trump the previous year by making obsolete those things that were once good enough, and then wonder why we aren't ever content with what we have. Giving gifts like a handmade afghan, a handwritten letter, or passing on our relished paperbacks is laughable against this backdrop of getting and gifting.

Turning inward amid the holiday frenzy presents more of a challenge. Continuous looping advertisements and promotions declaring yet another "biggest sale of the year" only add mounting pressure for us to play and pay along. There's little emphasis on the personal gifts we are already in a position to give—the ones that would cost us little to nothing—were we courageous enough to share them.

As a result, we spend less time thinking for ourselves, telling our own stories, making our own gifts, or developing anything of substance or meaning during the holiday season. Our newer models of happiness have now become inextricably linked with our ability to consume rather than create. Scarier even is we've become further detached from the truly urgent matters that affect others beyond the borders we've naturally drawn around our own heightened selves. We turn our gaze away from these matters with intolerance and indifference, in much of the same way we might ward off an unwelcome panhandler standing outside our car door asking for spare change while we wait anxiously for the light to turn green. We dismiss the inner voice that calls us to "greater", though we know that, fundamentally, something is off-kilter during this season. We know that this game, in which we've become willing pawns, has lost its focus and has become excessive. Though we hear that small voice within, we ignore it.

Once the events of the holiday season have ended, we're left asking "What now?" The merchandise that we couldn't afford before Christmas, but insisted on having, will be significantly discounted, and we feel foolish that we were so hell-bent on having them. "Clearance" and "All Items Must Go" replace "For Sale" signs; all items must go because there's more inventory than there are people left to buy it. The joke is always on us like an unsuspecting hidden camera.

Meanwhile, that same panhandler still goes hungry, food pantries in several households become further depleted, and folks who struggle to make ends meet every day still contend with meeting their basic needs beyond Christmas. Children continue to be abused by undetected family members and accosted by child predators. Politicians continue to drag their feet on programs that can bring relief to many a sufferer, and churchgoers continue to be lulled to sleep by prosperity preachers and other ne'er-do-wells. The thrill is gone. The novelty has worn off. There's no more shine and no more things to buy ... at least for now.

I am convinced that if we were to treat ourselves with the quiet and stillness during this holiday season, we'd find an inner joy that never grows old. More than the happiness that comes from a new gift, joy is deeply seated, intrinsic, and sustaining. That inward journey alone is far more exhilarating and rewarding that the novelty of any material possession we could ever buy; like finding a rare flower along the riverbanks just when we think we can travel no further. It is in that time, and through the stillness that our truly important gifts can be revealed or shared.

MY SISTER, MY SELF

New Lessons for My Daughters

Do you treasure the rare opportunity you get to catch up with someone you've known, but haven't spoken to or seen in quite a while? Though the two of you don't speak as often, you find yourself still connecting with each other as if the two of you had been friends all your life. I'm not sure we began as friends in high school, but thanks to social media, we were able to reconnect as grown women, without the banter and silliness that often characterizes the years between ages fourteen to eighteen, when we first met.

This friend was not among the few women with whom I remained connected since high school; however, our distinct journeys of motherhood, marriage, and life in general, connected us in ways that needed no explanation. We had taken different paths, yet the stops along the way were easily recognizable as we compared notes. Ultimately, we were at similar places in our self-development, which made the connection a timely one.

I have a few friendships like this one; collectively, they've become the backbone of what I refer to as my sisterhood, an extraordinary network of amazingly talented women, each enterprising and gifted on her own. This small sisterhood enriches, encourages, and sustains in ways that romantic and familial relationships cannot. Whether giving advice, lending expertise, or simply sharing their experience, there is a tremendous amount of reciprocity in terms of what each party is willing to bring to or take away from the table. In these relationships, I feel valued and trusted, and I arrive at the understanding that until now, I had been *mis*-educated or otherwise poorly informed about the relevance and necessity of sisterhood.

I grew up in a family where I did not witness strong or affirming relationships between my mother and other women.

I was taught, though not always explicitly, that women were not to be trusted, that relationships with them weren't worth the effort. Naturally, this perspective informed the way I viewed myself in the company of other women, and as a premise, I did not overtly seek to develop relationship with women. In fact, I reserved a special brand of cynicism on the subject of sisterhood, and never really thought about how this behavior might impact my own daughters, if I were to have any.

Two daughters later, though not necessarily because of them, I'm convinced that a sisterhood of women is essential for women to thrive. Rather than shun the idea of sisterhood, women should deliberately forge relationships with other women. This isn't to say that women should force friendships to exist where they don't exist, but rather, that they should make a conscientious effort to develop and nurture relationships that offer the potential for individual growth and further self-actualization. Ultimately, establishing relationships with other women should be a natural extension of us, much like talking to an old friend after a long time and picking up where you ended. Also, connection among women should be effortless when we are also rooted in something greater— somehow connected to a broader life purpose or service with which we can identify collectively. When the desire to grow as a result of these connections supersedes our individual needs for self-preservation and ego, authentic relationships can and do emerge.

I hope to provide my daughters with examples of authentic relationship and a newer and more accurate depiction of what sisterhood looks like. While I don't have the ability to rewrite my earlier lessons on sisterhood, I can write volumes for them through lived experiences. My ability to nurture and fortify the relationships with the women in my own life will be the ultimate proving ground. Certainly, my daughters will come to rely on each other as sisters, but I want them to also understand that thriving in this world as women—and not simply surviving—will require meaningful relationships with each other at all times.

Woman Wisdom

It wasn't even high noon yet, but dinner was already halfway cooked. Loads of laundry were washing and drying. I had written, was showered and dressed, and my house was clean. I had even responded to a few voicemail and email messages, was caught up on some outstanding reading, and had been quiet just long enough to be afforded some revelations. I had a pretty good idea of what I needed to do that day as well as a solid plan for getting it done. I even squeezed in some quality time with my hubby! But of course, a woman never reveals all the secrets that make her man smile.

Before you say "too much information," you should understand that there's nothing bawdy about romance. With the one you love, intimacy is to be treasured, written and sung about, and even savored like that last bite of dessert that you finally allowed yourself to have. And heck, if that someone who has brought a smile to your face happens to be you, then that's all good too!

This elixir of love, domestic life, personal connection and accomplishment, romance, and family is at the heart of what's important in life; I call them heart matters. So, what good is it then to only share the commonplace and predictable routine elements about relationship? In addition to being concerned with matters of my household and child rearing, I am first a woman with a full range of sensibilities as well as sensualities.

I'm hardly prudish, but I am private. I prefer to not hear the sordid details of someone else's messy love, though I do revel in the celebration of love. My unapologetic stance with regards to how much I choose to share has to do with a coming-of-age and acceptance of my womanhood. I feel a remarkable sense of ownership for my thoughts and truths, regardless of how they are received, and I am not afraid of disagreement.

My ownership as woman does not suggest a callous repudiation or dismissal of how others choose to share their love, but rather, a quiet wisdom gained from experience. Furthermore, my unbridled truth when shared, is informed by a faith that has sustained me this far, an intuition that feels divine, and a conviction of purpose and gifts that is aligned with something far greater than worldly appetites to bare and see all. I will not share simply for the sake of sharing. With this ownership comes the important job of boundary setting. I know what I am willing to do and not do, and there's really no point trying to get me to do otherwise. I am also more discerning of the intentions and motivations of others, though I don't need to scrutinize them.

All of this makes for a more contemplative, introspective, and oft quieter time. The goal is not to isolate myself; however, should I find that I am one of only a few in my convictions, I'm okay with that. I'm learning that though I am a people person, I really do enjoy my own company. I'm good with me, and me alone. Feels just right, if you ask me. Like that last piece of dessert, I fully intend to savor the wisdom that comes with this season of my becoming.

Painting a Picture:
On Race & Identity

I want something beautiful
Blooming
something to nurture
and till
and cultivate
with good soil
bountiful crop
trees tall ... and fruitful hope.
Ain't none of that 'roun here.

—AVRIL SOMERVILLE,
A Return to 'Normalcy'?

Welcome to America

There's no easy way for me to speak of race, so when I was asked to write for the PBS Race 2012 Blogging Project during President Barack Obama's campaign for a second term, I found myself contemplating my most salient introduction of race as both a construct and as part of what would become a larger part of my identity as a Black woman in America. Let's just say, my world wasn't always black and white.

When I migrated to Brooklyn, New York from the Commonwealth of Dominica in the West Indies at the age of ten, I never anticipated that America would be so fragmented along the lines of race and class. Unlike America, my homeland of Dominica was a small island that even people from the rest of the Caribbean islands referred to as too small to be considered significant, unlike the larger and more well-known island countries of Haiti or Jamaica. Dominica was not the same place as the more familiar Dominican Republic, but an English-speaking island still young in its independence from a British colonial regime in 1978.

Dominica was a proud place with even prouder people, a place where there was more talk about its music and cricket but little open talk about race in terms of Black versus White. During the time that I lived there, one was either classified as Dominican or foreigner, regardless of skin color. Of course, there was broader talk of "oppression" in the context of colonization and further threat of imperialism veiled beneath foreign aid from other countries, but our living there was not racialized, per se.

There, my knowledge of race came primarily from the Bob Marley songs that my uncle would blare urging Africa to unite, heralding Paul Bogle, threatening revolution, denouncing colonization, and promising liberation. From these songs, I quickly gathered that colonized people all over the African

Diaspora were marginalized at the hands of a common White oppressor and were made to believe themselves as inferior based on their skin color alone.

Moving to New York, I was catapulted into a racially charged environment where lines were clearly defined according to race. Some of the fiercest criticism I encountered came from people who looked much like me, yet took every opportunity to remind me of what they saw as difference. At school, my accent sounded strange, my clothes were certainly not in season, and getting free lunch was ridiculed, though it appeared that most of us qualified. I felt like I had been thrown to the wolves to fend for myself. Though I was clearly Black by all appearances, I did not feel the "Black Power" or the love, and certainly not the community that we would share in the identification of a common oppressor. For whatever reason, it seemed that my Black American community looked down on my immigrant status and cared little about my desire to also partake in the American dream. As if adjusting to a new environment weren't sufficient, I had to accept my new minority status of immigrant within an already clearly identified minority, whether I wanted to or not. I also had to deal with a complex set of new problems including institutionalized racism, navigating within my newer margins of Black America, and the age-old "immigrant versus American" debate.

Clearly, being a Black immigrant from the Caribbean in a predominantly Black American community coupled with a backdrop of already painful race relations in America did not give me an advantage. I went from being a native in Dominica to a foreigner in the U.S. and picked up new labels and class affiliations including "inner city," "minority," "at risk," "other," "disadvantaged," and even "Haitian" by peers who thought it more convenient to lump all people from the Caribbean into one island. Skin color and common class experiences alone were not sufficient to establish the new bonds that I would need to feel at home in my new home.

Beyond my social context, I gleaned that there was a much more concerted effort to institutionalize Blacks from the Caribbean as African-Americans. Although we did not choose these labels for ourselves, the boxes were already demarcated as convenient for some, and we were forced to ascribe to the most obvious. I did not feel a sense of belonging among my Black neighbors or classmates, yet I had no desire—and still don't—to be anywhere else. I wanted to belong, though I didn't feel welcome just then, hence began my relationship with race.

PAINTING A PICTURE: ON RACE & IDENTITY

Ode to Troy Davis/Affected

Denied!
Justice?
Stay? No stay.

3/5?
Perhaps less.
Miscarriage?
Worse. Execution.

Stillborn within me
Indescribable emotion
Lie in wait for the mercy of man.

Boiling.
Seething.
Feeling…
Helpless.
Hurting.
Hardly living
In a post-racial
Era eclipsed by illusions of justice, empathy, or righteousness.

I'm left asking
Wanting
Needing
Answers to address "destiny."
Whose destiny is it?
When man decides the fate of who stays, and
who will expire?

Men wrought with
Haunting emotions, and
Erasable scars of
Premature and wrongful visits by their dispensation of death's
sting.

Is it only in death that love will be reunited?
One, with another?
Until then,
Sisters
Mothers
Brothers
Children wail
Bellyaching sorrow.

No room for redress?

I beg
Believing my God will intervene.
But my prayers fell like heavy rain on fallen leaves,
Only to evaporate and
Consumed by a vicious cycle of news spin, new news, and
eroded sensibilities.

For Troy Davis. DOD: 21 September 2011 11:08 pm EST

Massive Cover-Up

Under this thin veil of a sheet
My body feels bruised, battered, and beat.
Worn down by the hardest fight of my life,
I can but barely breathe.

Still in a state of unconsciousness,
But ever so slightly aware.
In between stages of out and in,
I'm not quite sure how I got here.

Will God take me now, hushed as might be?
This, I know can't be His will.
How much more can this yearning for life
Torment, ride, and taunt me still?

No one comes to claim me lest I die,
No turning back, not now it seems.
Can't hold on much longer…still…I try,
Figured by now, this ain't no dream.

I lie at heaven's gate,
It's too somber, too surreal.
My body feels weightless,
My soul flees somewhere to keep.

Can't catch a break, not even a breath.
This vacuum of horror,
This stench of death.
Family, home, what else have I left?

Behind…me, I hear a calvary,
A throng of criers, mothers, groan.
Mourning what sounds like a weeping song,
Children, fathers, aunts, preachers moan.

They cover me with their promise of love,
And cloak me with their vow.
That history cannot repeat itself,
Too much at stake right now.

I shut my eyes this one last time,
I know there won't be a revival
For me…but for many scores more,
I'll have to wait for their arrival.

I've fought this march to the bitter end,
Yet death won't loosen its grip.
So until the death knell rings for them,
My life will kindle their wick.

For Trayvon Martin DOD: 26 February 2012. Age: 17

In Search of Our Wiz

One night, our family sat down to watch *The Wiz*. I had never truly watched *The Wiz*. I had a few good reasons. For starters, we did not own a television. I was still living in my native country of Dominica in the West Indies and by the time I arrived to the United States four years later, it was already out of theatres and off the air. Moreover, by all accounts, we were a West Indian family who did not make a big deal about being Black in America. So here I was, at the age of forty, giddy with delight, about finally seeing *The Wiz* for the first time.

I was already familiar with the powerhouse that is Stephanie Mills and her unbridled performance of "Home" in the Broadway musical of the same name, but I didn't know that *The Wiz* was an adaptation of *The Wizard of Oz*, a musical fantasy film produced in 1939. Both were inspired by L. Frank Baum's children's book, *The Wonderful Wizard of Oz*. Rather than retelling the plot or story lines, I'll share some of what inspired me about this adaptation.

My first reaction was simply that this could not have been a remake; this was a major production. Replete with explosive choreography, musical talent, and top-shelf performers including Quincy Jones, Diana Ross, Nipsey Russell, Ted Ross, Lena Horne, Michael Jackson, and Richard Pryor, *The Wiz* did not disappoint. I even had to give Diana Ross some credit for bringing her own verve and passion to her rendition of "Home." Just when you thought her small frame of a body was going to blow over, she would dig deep and play such a convincing Dorothy that one would think she was delivering her personal story.

Seeing *The Wiz* piqued my curiosity about the perceptions we have about access. Who has the power to grant access and why do we ask for it? Are all barriers to access real or are some imagined, based on other factors like fear, past experience, insecurity about our own adequacy, or some unique combination of those?

Each and every time the main characters Dorothy, Tinman, Scarecrow, or Lion (aka Fleetwood Coupe de Ville) would hail for a cab, the light atop the taxi would register an off-duty sign. Was that symbolic or coincidental? I interpreted "off duty" as "access denied." Rather than being able to enjoy the comfort or convenience of getting a ride, Dorothy and her crew had to "ease on down the road," on foot yet again, but only after they used those cabs as bridges, climbing and dancing all over them to make further headway along their journey. It was as if Dorothy and her friends were saying, "Fine, we'll make our own way." Suddenly, the song "Ease On Down the Road," sung by the younger and popular Michael Jackson, signified something much more personal and political. The silent protest in the actions of Dorothy and her crew did not go unnoticed. It is interesting that, even now, so many of us find ourselves having to forge our own access.

The Wiz was also a cautionary tale about not assigning too much authority or value to Wiz characters. The Wiz, played by Richard Pryor, was no exception. Behind the seemingly indestructible mask, he was a lonely and fraudulent man with a broken spirit. He too, was hurt by life's disappointments, and had his own personal limitations. He had no clue how to get Dorothy home, much less get anyone else a heart, brain, or courage. In fact, this Wiz was hardly decisive about much.

The main characters in *The Wiz* shared insecurities about their worth and abilities, but in their collective journey down the yellow brick road, they found a sense of community. By all appearances, the Tinman only needed some mechanical work, though what he expressed was the need for a heart to grant him the capacity to love and feel. Scarecrow wanted a brain or intellect, but what he really lacked was confidence and credibility in his own ideas. Lion, of all people, needed courage. Just as in life, those who appear to be the strongest are often in need of just as much affirmation and encouragement as anyone else. Lastly, Dorothy just wanted to get back home.

But where was home? When Dorothy sang, she referred to

a place where "there's love overflowing." Away from home, however, she learned of yet a different kind of love. The words of her song imparted that the energy we expend trying to find and settle into places called home might insulate us from the real world, where love is hardly abundant, and certainly not always unconditional. Though Dorothy still yearned for a place called home, she emphasized the importance of finding home within ourselves and not so much in the physical places that life might take us.

During my adolescence, I reminisced about my childhood home in Dominica. While there, the wingspan of my grandmother's arms would protect me from storms, real or imagined. It was her covering of love that would shield me from the colder realities I would encounter in my new environment called New York City. Not having that assurance in my new "home" often made me feel displaced, insecure, and uncertain. In this unknown city of bright lights, taxicabs, and shysters, I would search for my Wiz. Unknowingly, some of these so-called Wiz characters preyed on my naïveté. In my quest for belonging, they would do and say anything to make me feel at home, and I too, played a role in assigning them value that they neither earned nor deserved.

Much of my insecurity arose not from needing a Wiz, but from my own real fears about making the wrong decisions, or taking the wrong path. It took some difficult experiences and broken relationships along the way for me to learn that life was less about making the wrong choices, and more about owning the consequences of those choices. Releasing that fear of being wrong led me to that place called "home," a metaphor for my happiness, which made searching for a Wiz not only irrelevant, but futile.

Jumping Rope Alone

As a girl growing up in New York City, I often found myself on the sidelines of many a Double Dutch game. I was what other girls called "double-handed"—incapable of simultaneously turning the two long ropes in opposite directions—while yet another girl jumped in rhythm between them, over the sounds of chanting or cheering onlookers and rope turners. I desperately wanted to jump because, as a younger child in the West Indies. I jumped rope regularly with schoolmates during recess and outdoor play; however, there was no such thing as Double Dutch in my loving community of Goodwill, Dominica. There, we had a variety of games that involved jumping or "skipping" with a single rope. My friends would turn the rope, lifting it higher with each new attempt for me to jump over it to the other side. Other times, we'd jump with our single rope, carefree and rhythmically, just before the rope would skim the ground beneath our tennis shoes.

Double Dutch was something entirely different to me in my new, hardscrabble Brooklyn neighborhood. The urgency of life was palpable and unbending. This setting was in sharp contrast to the more relaxed and forgiving pace that characterized my life growing up in the West Indies. The patience required for someone to teach me and for me to learn the fundamentals of Double Dutch, was scarce among adolescent girls where I lived in Brooklyn. I made the mistake of assuming that the girls who played Double Dutch would appreciate our common delight for jumping rope, and naturally, would help me scale the learning curve, but they just wanted to get back to their fun, not waste time teaching me. I wanted so badly to jump in the hot summer sun, even if I had to do it alone, but was consumed by the fear of looking silly with my solitary rope jumping off to the side by myself, but now…

Now as an adult, I not only jump alone, but I jump often. Just me with my jump rope, without the running commentary and snickering about my lack of skills. Just me, without a care in the world about who's watching, regardless of where I am. With my headphones on and my favorite jams in rotation, I jump, squat, jack, lunge, and do whatever I please, with each turn of the rope.

The rope goes over my head and under my feet as I keep pace, remembering to breathe the entire time—in through the nose, out through the mouth. Knees tucked near my chest at times, soles sometimes grazing my bottom, I continue to jump. I keep the rhythm as I try to beat my last interval, and grow eager to see how much longer I can jump each new chance I get before I trip my feet again in the rope. I emerge from the rope, catch my breath, and feel the throb of every heartbeat. I feel like such a child again, like I've conquered that Double Dutch thing after all, like I've won a small personal victory inside.

Who needs Double Dutch when singles will do? There is immense joy and pleasure in play, even as a grownup, even when you're alone. Give yourself permission to play again. Reconnect with your inner child and honor that space, for it is indeed sacred, insomuch that it extracts an unparalleled joy and nostalgia that reaffirms exactly who you have always been.

Enough

Cringing at the thought that what I pour
Into my 15-year-old Black son is not enough
That despite
The discipline with which I rear him
The love with which I affirm him
The pride with which I love him
The way in which I've taught him
Won't be enough
If some desperate, entitled soul feels one day that
Perhaps he…
Walks too proudly
Answers too definitively
Speaks too haughtily
Smiles too brightly
Listens to his music too loudly
I am afraid that the love with which both of us have raised him
is simply not enough
That despite
Steeping and brewing him in faith
and love
and worth
and childhood
and young manhood
The sum of all of this is still not enough.

Yearning: Once a Mother, Twice a Child

I am slowly freeing you from me
releasing into the wind
that which I don't want to become
that which I see keeps me in an unhealthy place
that which seeks to weigh down on my chest so heavily.
I will never succumb to its pressure
for that's too heavy a burden.

I am stronger.

—Avril Somerville,
Breathing

Loosing and Finding Love ... Unconditional

In one of his weekly addresses titled "Celebrating Fathers," President Barack Obama spoke of the necessary building blocks of fatherhood, including quality time and structure. He also emphasized the importance of unconditional love. His message really got me thinking about parenting in general, and in particular about the 'unconditional love' part that is required to raise well-adjusted children with a healthy sense of self-worth, discernment, and empathy in today's environment.

Titling this essay "Loosing and Finding Love ... Unconditional" seems most appropriate because it best captures the full engagement that is required to identify, receive, and ultimately give love. This spectrum of transformation is the current that undergirds my journey as a mother and as a citizen of this larger human circle. Parenting not only requires that we manage the layers of distractions to deliver focused messages and attention to our children, but that we loosen—deconstruct and confront—issues of the self on an ongoing basis. It's no wonder that I find myself constantly sorting through the tapes of my upbringing to understand how they inform me as a person, and by extension, examining whether their impact limits or empowers me to be an even better parent.

As a child, my family's opinion was my primary filter. My parents and grandparents made choices that they believed to be in my best interest, while not sacrificing their own. What they said and did—or didn't, mattered heavily to me, almost to a fault. So naturally, when they were less than affirming or validating, it mattered. I wanted to know that they would love me no matter what. I wanted them to embrace me no matter what or who I became and even when my opinions or actions fell outside their views or expectations. When the goal of their instruction was to make me more independent or build a thick skin, it only resulted in a greater emotional distance that became more difficult to close. Furthermore, when the exchanges lacked the intimacy that I needed to feel valued, it also mattered greatly. Though the dysfunction of these truths didn't register with me until later in life, I now realize that I struggled not only with my sense of belonging and self-worth as a child, but also with what it meant to give and receive unconditional love well into my adult life.

As I continue to work through these truths in my daily living and learning, I have to consciously work to bridge those gaps because ultimately I want to be closer and more accessible to my own children. That isn't easy. I've come to learn that before I can impart unconditional love to my children, I first have to acknowledge and release those difficult truths because they prevent me from fully loving or receiving love. Though undoubtedly necessary, unpacking my emotional baggage is painful; however, it is amazingly cathartic. In so doing, I'm learning that parenting is not a perfect science, but rather, a "responsible" art, whose outcome depends on many variables and repeated trial and error.

I believe that the only way to make sure that we're on the right track is to uncover that which continues to keep us bound or held captive to painful pasts or vicious cycles. Then finally, we must release or pry them "loose" from those places, because they keep us from receiving and giving unconditional love. Don't be fooled; this is not a one-time assignment, but rather, an ongoing process that requires lots of forgiveness … and controlled breathing. It isn't until then that we can name and model the behaviors that we seek in ourselves, let alone in our children. We can only be authentic with our children when we are transparent with ourselves. Once I've identified the problem and put it in its proper perspective and place, I'm learning that it's really okay to open up to my children; there's nothing they want more. Giving children structure and boundaries does not require us to be infallible, omniscient, or super resilient. Allowing ourselves to be vulnerable and human is paramount because we want them, one day, to open up and trust us, also. Giving ourselves permission to not be so thick-skinned that we come across as unaffected is both healthy and human; it is what connects us with them.

I'm learning to love without condition, to give my children my love simply because I've been blessed with their life, and because they need my unconditional love to evolve as self-confident, empathetic beings. I'm learning to give them my presence by engaging the many questions of their seeking. I'm learning to give them my love. As their maturity allows, I hope to continue to foster my own healing by sharing with them the most inconvenient truths of my own be-coming. I believe that in so doing, our children will understand more about life itself. We've got to make sure that they know we love and value them through intimate time spent together, exchanges, and other small acts of love, even when we disagree and they leave us scratching our heads. In the end, it won't be about whether we've molded perfection, but whether we have helped to shape and nurture the minds and hearts of those we ultimately release into the world, regardless of who or what they become. At the end of the day, it's all about the love … love unconditional.

YEARNING: ONCE A MOTHER, TWICE A CHILD

The Art of Raising Children

Raising children is more than a job. It is an art that takes no less than everything. To make this mosaic beautifully coordinated, every section, stage, or story must be carefully considered and arranged in such a way that, to the viewer, it appears harmonious, intricate, and yet deliberate. The resulting symphony should be music to one's ears, yet convey part pattern, and part rhyme and reason. It is definitely not a haphazardly strewn arrangement of gaudy pieces, inferior materials, or false maneuvers that can be covered by cutting corners. One cannot grow weary of weaving, or of the repetition of attempts to "get it right." Sometimes, it means unraveling what you thought was a finished piece and starting over. These are not exercises in futility; I assure myself. I realize that I am building a legacy, one that cannot stand on its own legs, but one that requires deliberate and thoughtful action, retrospective reflection, and the participation of all those involved in ensuring the masterpiece is brought to life.

This art of building a legacy for our children can be likened to making a quilt, or sewing a tapestry. It should reflect an intentional coordination of design, partnership of techniques, and care. Unlike a one-dimensional drawing, the goal in creating it is not that of achieving symmetry or perfection, but a depth that isn't readily appreciated by the untrained eye. This ancient art of raising children is worn and worsted, tried and true, and should reflect a carryover and integration of ancestral wisdom and experiences that have made the most beautiful of tapestries by the oldest and sturdiest of hands, yet depict some of the more modern adjustments and adaptations of newer techniques that are better suited for our current times. As a result, this work of art should contain the fundamental building blocks of what has worked in the past and what we continue to build upon in the present.

YEARNING: ONCE A MOTHER, TWICE A CHILD

Regardless of not knowing how it will all turn out in the end, we should continue to work on our masterpieces. Establishing and maintaining the goal of creating something beautiful gives us creative license and allows us the necessary focus and intention that the work deserves. Moreover, the precision with which we as parent artists can delve into each segment of our individual canvas allows us to leave our own indelible impressions. Rest assured that the resulting masterpiece will be more layered and textured than anything we could ever perceive or been taught.

What a Girl Wants

My oldest daughter—then five—had been asking me to blow dry her hair "straight" and give her bouncy curls for some time. Though it seemed like a simple request, I dreaded the amount of time and work that it would involve. Let me explain. My daughter has a very thick head of hair. It is very soft, but after it dries from washing, it can become an unruly mess. I ran through the mental checklist of all the reasons why she should wait, then I heard a small voice inside tugging at me to remember that every girl needs to feel special no matter what her age; to feel that she matters enough for someone to take the time, regardless of inconvenience, to love and to care for her. This is what a girl wants!

I grabbed her by the hand, reached for a bottle of no-tears shampoo, and began to wash her hair. I assured her that this would be the easy part. After the repeated patterns of sectioning, combing, drying, and moisturizing, I took to the delicate work of curling her hair with the heated curling irons. I wanted to be really careful to avoid burning her ears, skin, or hair. Then she said, "I don't just want my hair blow-dried and straight, Mom. I want it curled too. Like a princess!" She also wanted style and a little bit of pomp and circumstance.

What I wanted was not very different from what she wanted. It was a yearning for us to spend more special time together. Oddly enough, I felt like I was getting her ready for some big event. Would she like it? Would I be comfortable with seeing her look slightly more grown up? Would she ask me to do this more often than I'd care to? Would I then have to share with her my opinions on why she shouldn't have her hair like this more regularly? We got to talk about what was on her mind, and I got to revel in her excitement and anticipation about the big reveal, once we were finished.

Then a rather different mood hit me altogether. My mind

fast-forwarded to her teenage years and young adulthood, and the mirrors into which she may look as she morphs into her various stages of becoming the young woman that I imagine she will become—first day of middle school, high school, Sweet 16, prom, going off to college, her first heartbreak. My eyes held back the tears that stirred in my heart, and I became full with longing for her to return to her childhood, though she still sat before me as a five-year old. Each stroke of the hairbrush and release of a new Shirley Temple curl became that more deliberate and contemplative.

While I attended to her, I shared stories about my grandmother who would secure me between her knees to comb and grease my wild and woolly hair. I explained to her that though I appreciated my grandmother taking time with me, I wasn't too keen on the crookedly parted plaits and pigtails that I got after enduring all that pain. That just didn't feel like a fair deal. I was surprised by my daughter's sensitivity toward my grandmother, whom she had met at only six months old, an age too young to remember. I told her that had my grandmother been alive, she would scoff at the lengths I was going through to now elaborately style her hair, applying heat to such a tender head. Surely, this would result in her growing up too fast, my grandmother would maintain.

I contemplated how my five-year old would remember these moments we were spending together. Were my responses affirming? Was my touch gentle enough? Did I celebrate her, and more importantly, did we both share in the moment that I hoped would be bottled forever. I was doing my best to create what I hoped would be a sweet memory. She approached the mirror, looked at her hair, smiled at herself, and remarked, "I look beautiful, Mommy." Her words needed no chorus or response. Though I was happy to provide one, she was sure of it, as she continued to exchange smiles with her reflection; that was all that mattered.

My heart smiled, wider than my face could manage, as I held back tears of joy. She felt confident, radiant, and beautiful! I hoped that she would hold on to this remarkable confidence and always see herself as worthy of her Mommy's love and care, without hearing "next week," or "maybe tomorrow." From her, I now understood that every little girl needs to feel that they matter enough for someone to take the time, love, nurture and care with them. "Every girl needs to feel special, no matter what their age."

When I Grow up, I Want to Be a Mommy

My youngest daughter, who wasn't quite four, blurted those words one morning as I fastened her into her car seat, rather hurriedly I might add. She pronounced this aspiration so matter-of-factly it was as if she had just had a quiet epiphany. It wasn't the first time that I had heard those words, but for some reason, their unsolicited and random delivery totally took me off guard this time. Despite my hurriedness, I could see by the tenderness of my daughter's eyes that she was sincere. Moreover, the certainty of her words made me think more deeply about their meaning and the questions that they elicited in me.

Did she mean it in the same way that another child might say that she wants to be a doctor or a writer? Or, is Mommy simply one of the many roles that she'd like to play when she grows up, much in the same way that she wants to be a Cheerleader-Princess-Ballerina-Rockstar? What did she mean by "I Want to Be A Mommy," and why did the statement give me such pause?

I was reluctant to ask her directly because, after all, she couldn't possibly grasp the significance of my emotions or questioning; but more importantly, because I was afraid that her answers might tarnish what felt like a really beautiful moment for me just then. What if she said something hurtful like "Mommies get to stay home and watch TV all day and never have to work?" Or worse yet, what if she reduced being a mommy to the tangible chores and routines that she saw me do regularly, versus the broader and more meaningful significance that I ascribe to motherhood?

The last thing I wanted to hear was my daughter make light of what it means to be a mother, which might be different still from what she characterizes as "mommy." Had I prompted her, she may have said something remarkably beautiful or affirming like "I want to be a mommy because mommies love and take such good care of their children"; however, I never gave her that opportunity. In order to protect myself and because of my fear and insecurity about the answers, I left the pronouncement suspended and sealed it off from further discussion.

I took great joy in the possibility that my daughter's excitement might be due, at least in part, to something that I must be doing right, but I couldn't help projecting my personal concerns and struggles with becoming a mom, and the larger issue of women identification and value being heavily tied to motherhood. I know that my daughter is still young, and that there will be several more iterations of what she wants to be when she grows up, yet I couldn't help but wonder whether in my choosing to be home with my children, especially my daughters, I was implying that other options were not worth considering, or conversely, that being a mommy should be their singular and most important desire.

My eldest daughter, however, who is three years older, has since clarified what she meant by those same words, which she also uttered around the same age. She's a bit more deliberate and careful with her words and hence, mommy's ego, but still I marveled when she emphatically declared that, "Mommy is just one of the things that I'd like to be when I grow up, as well as being an artist, and a preacher." The pursuit of motherhood at the expense of suppressing her natural gifts of prayer and praise, and creativity and design, is simply not an option for her. She seems to already understand on some level, that they go hand in hand in making her the consummate young woman that she wishes to become.

Naturally, I will have more elaborate discussions with my children as their maturity allows, but in the meantime I wonder what messages they take away from my prioritization of their care, in my choosing to be home with them. Certainly, there are a host of interests that I pursue outside of being their mom, but foremost in their mind is "Mommy" as it relates to caring for them. Maybe "Mommy" for them captures all that I am and do, but perhaps more appropriately, it is that I am their constant, or even more prophetically, I am a guardian for their care and a keeper of my promise to protect and to love them unconditionally.

Certainly, there is tremendous value and great joy in being a "Mommy," especially within the context of marriage, where the relationship is built on trust and a mutual respect between two people that are aligned and fully committed to the care of their children. I would like to believe that for my daughters, the impression of being a Mommy has something to do with this context; otherwise, I'm not so certain that they would romanticize motherhood. Nonetheless, I want them to understand that their self-worth is not tied to their ability to marry, or carry or birth children, but rather, to the legacies and meaning that they create in their own lives and communities, whether they become preachers, artists, Cheerleader-Princess-Ballerina-Rockstars, mommies, or even none of the above.

YEARNING: ONCE A MOTHER, TWICE A CHILD

For Them, Not Us

I lay restlessly on my bed one night, considering the event that got me there. My then five-year-old daughter had been struggling to design and to draw a dress. As she set out to create her masterpiece, she would become increasingly frustrated with each attempt. With papers strewn about, she threw down her pencil, and demanded to know why she just couldn't "get it!" Her arms were good and folded, her lips poked out, and her tears began in earnest. Her insistence on an explanation as to why she was struggling blew my mind.

What audacity of me to recommend that she look at some of the dresses in her closet as inspiration, or peruse a magazine to help guide her in the process. She scoffed at the notion that she would need to do that, and insisted that she didn't want to create anything based on something that had already been done. How dare I suggest something so ridiculous? "That would be copying, Mom. I am a self-made artist!," she protested. Fair enough I thought, for I certainly didn't know what to make of this latest meltdown. I'm usually quick on my feet, able to craft a response of some kind to my children's dilemmas, but this time, I was dumbfounded.

Art, for my daughter was like breathing—something she did almost always, something that staved off boredom, a special space where she seemed to be quite comfortable without the need for anything more. Art held her captive from the time she was fifteen months, when she drew her first smiley face, which floated at the right corner of her page, with eyes askance. By age two, the smiley faces were replaced real people and not stick figures. Her portfolio would expand to include various types of art, but the one thing that was consistent in all of her art was their lifelikeness, vibrancy and color. She almost always had a story to share behind the art— one that would convey human intentions, dispositions, and reactions to something relatable in the world of the subject, which she seemed to capture so brilliantly and seemingly effortlessly, in some form or another.

As parents, we struggle when our children are challenged by something new; however, that something new is only new to us. Oftentimes, this new thing is something about which they are most passionate, but we don't always understand or see it the way they do, hence the difficulty in crafting our response. The best thing we can do in those instances is to empathize while quietly affirming them. We can simply avail ourselves to our children as a soundboard without the need to have an answer because there isn't always one. Let them navigate a bit and arrive at their own conclusions. They will eventually find the answers that they need and when they do, they will be grateful that we were simply there—present without being overbearing or all-knowing, seeking to give definition to something that only experience can explain.

Purposeful Intentions

The revitalizing
The restoring
The covering
You know what I'm talking about
Those pretty ten
'Dem calloused, rough-hewn ten
Those still very useful
Ten

—AVRIL SOMERVILLE,
Lend Ten

Go on, Open the Present

The saying goes that most of us are only one situation away from a drastically different reality. When you hear this, the first thing that comes to mind is usually of a financial nature. We immediately consider how different life would be if we were to lose our jobs or the ability to meet our basic needs; however, there are situations other than the loss of our jobs that can upend reality as we know it. Some of these situations might include a new medical diagnosis that eats away at our savings—should we have any—the untimely death of a loved one, or the sudden need to shoulder the responsibility of caring for an additional person. Rather than think of these situations as adverse events, I'd like to reimagine them as life changes and seasons, possibly signaling the turning of a new leaf.

Sometimes, those we love might view our responses as shallow or even detached if we ourselves are not dealing with the same difficult circumstances. Though I would like to believe that I am in tune with them, sufficiently so to know when they are thrown off-kilter by something more personal and looming, I often feel limited in my ability to offer exactly the kind of help they might need. The knowledge that my time and resources paled in such comparison to the need, offered me little consolation.

I grew concerned about the growing embarrassment and shame that a mother might feel about not being able to feed her children, let alone buy them something special during the holidays. I felt an affinity for fathers seized with worry about job security; and envisioned bedrooms with children needing ongoing medical and emotional attention. On their beds, I would perch spiritual mothers who, by extending their hands alone, could render magical healing powers on my behalf. I wanted to be with all of these persons and situations all at once, but could not. I felt a heavy burden about not being able to cast my net wide enough to help.

Perhaps it was my own late grandmother guiding me through these internal heart visits, because these images hardly felt concocted or contrived. Even after years of making her physical transition from this earth, I found her spirit remarkably close to me, almost coexisting with me on my most reflective days. She reminded me often about what really matters—that our brethren should not be found so deprived of what they need or too depraved in spirit to carry on. These visions were so visceral that they awakened in me a simultaneous sense of urgency and guilt, as well as a tremendous gratitude for my own blessings.

Reconciling this dichotomy became an obsession that riddled me especially during the holidays, but talking about such macabre matters never seemed to bode well for dinner conversation. Before the conversation could even get underway, I was reminded to keep the upbeat spirit of Christmas. I, on the other hand, thought the holiday season was a perfectly appropriate occasion to consider how we can serve. It is during this period of excess that the indulgences are seen for what they really are, especially in contrast to those without the basics. Apart from these times of the year, I'm not sure that the comparisons are as glaring, or the situations as bleak. Revisiting holiday traditions that include outlandish gift buying, expensive decorating, overeating, and wastefulness, all which take us away from our core values is an exercise that we must do regularly if we say we desire to live truly examined lives. We can no longer keep traditions for the sake of tradition when our inner moral compass convicts us otherwise. When we know better, we should do better.

We can begin by clearing our plates a bit, to allow our schedules and minds the space we need to nurture the compassion that I believe most of us inherently have. Left with more quality time, we can be more attentive to others who need us, starting with our own friends and family. Just think of the prospects of being able to check in on folk year-round, and not just during the holidays! Though this work requires some sacrifice, everyone's load will be a little bit lighter for it, and we'd all be healthier.

Sadly enough, one doesn't have to go very far to identify someone in need of our presence. Sadness, stress, and depression are not confined to zip code, class, or household, but our active listening is required if we are to actually hear both the spoken and unspoken "cries" for help in our midst. We may not have the complete solution, but we can be of some help. If we are guided by spirit and the truth of our convictions, we can help create the safe spaces or opening that one needs for their own restoration.

It is important to remember that people will always remember your sincerity and the spirit of your intentions. Moreover, they will appreciate that you took the time from your busy life to care, that you made them a priority. Our human presence uplifts the soul, so rather than buying another present, simply be more present.

PURPOSEFUL INTENTIONS

This Whole Lenten Business

Every Lenten season, I find myself in a quandary about what I should abstain from, and whether I should even participate at all. Though my faith suggests that I would benefit from this season of preparation just before Easter, I wasn't quite sure that my playing along made that much of a difference. Until then, these forty days of abstinence seemed more about proving to the world one's ability to adhere to a discipline or habit during a time that is designed for personal reflection and spiritual growth. I'm still not sure how giving up ice cream or chocolate for forty days helps anyone but the person who is fasting. Perhaps such restraint does help the family's grocery bill, but beyond that, the jury is still out.

One particular Lenten season, I decided to take a bit of a social media hiatus. Readapting the oft-cited SMH acronym––typically used online to indicate, "shaking my head"––to mean social media hiatus, seemed entirely appropriate at the time. It was a subversion of sorts—my understanding of what really needed to happen with me in order for me to be fully present and prepared for any spiritual restoration or renewal, including Easter.

Disengaging entirely from social media for this forty-day period and being intentional in the time I claimed to be spending with family, self, and with the responsibility of honoring my gifts—including my writing—would be time well spent. During this time, I got to celebrate a dear friend's birthday and thoroughly enjoyed being in her presence. I met several of her friends for the first time, but focused less on my being the odd woman out, simply because I love her. I spent time with yet another friend, got up to speed on her life, and exchanged notes on our personal challenges of managing our respective creative outlets while still being good wives and mothers.

Reconnecting separately with both friends during this Lenten season was not only meaningful, but also instructive. The experience was a reminder to check in more often. Furthermore, it allowed me to tap into an emotional center that can only be intimately nurtured in person, in the absence of the distraction of social media. Put simply, there is no substitute for good conversation and time with a few good friends.

Away from friends and at home, I had the added bonus of interacting more patiently with, and listening more intently to, my children. When my son called home to negotiate more time playing basketball in exchange for picking up his sisters from the bus—because it would "give you more time to write, Mom"—I simply obliged; I really did not mind his every pleading word. I listened more attentively to both his, and his sisters' unspoken words, and sensed their appreciation for the hands-free attention I was finally giving them.

I sat right across from my sweetheart more often than not. Even when we were not engaged in conversation, we were happy just being together. Being undistracted and available should he need me was all he seemed to have wanted, and I didn't mind indulging him.

Lastly, I had more time to tend to me, in more mindful ways, without any chocolate or ice cream restrictions. There was more time to capture and write down those thoughts before they evaporated into yet another online comment, Tweet, or Facebook status. It seemed that this particular year, the Lenten season was aligned perfectly with my need for reflection and intimate connection with the more constant joys of life—friends and family, community. While I understand the significance of fasting and abstinence, I think that spending more time being mindful and connected during Lent—a more turning inward of the soul to spirit, so to speak—more accurately honors the sanctity of Lent, beyond prescribed times on any calendar, while being respectful of those who may not observe Lent.

Mark My Words

As I listened to my workout playlist one morning, I gave thought to the myriad ways we use our voice, and how much of an impact our choices have in affecting human outcomes. I think many of us underestimate the power of our voice, but there is so much potential there; with it, we can coalesce forces, or dig a divide; we can build consensus, or add to the discord of despair; we can inspire hope, or join the dispirited harmony of the hopeless; we can lift someone's spirit, or add to the singsong of the naysayers. The world awaits the melody of this precious gift of an instrument, which most of us have the ability to use.

We can whisper encouragement or render a kind affirmation. We can hum a sweet melody or sing a beautiful song. We can speak with a conviction that others may need to hear during particularly difficult times of their lives. In essence, we can be a voice for others, a vessel, a perfectly tuned instrument, carrying what someone else may need for just that moment.

The choices are endless, but this isn't to suggest that our voices should only be used to keep the peace. It is important that we also use our voices to express our outrage, and to incite action on behalf of those without the privilege or position to do so. You can still say what you need to say without using your words as weapons; however, it's equally important that you choose what you say before offering up what you believe is wisdom or insight. Unfortunately and too often, we speak without thinking. Sometimes, our words are measured, deliberate, and carefully ensconced in political correctness and sensitivity so as not to offend, but too often, we say whatever we want, through the non-meditations of our heart, insecurities, and past hurts.

I consider the various occasions that I've heard words

exchanged between so-called loved ones in public places, hurled across a room with the force of a weighted object, all with the intention of rendering an honest opinion. The assailant achieves his ends, albeit it at the expense of tearing down the targeted recipient. Sometimes the heated exchange is followed by apologetic pleas and requests for forgiveness, but by then the damage is done. Seeds of judgment, shame, betrayal, or other undiscovered inadequacy have already taken a hold. The guilty party may also be hurt and remorseful, not necessarily for the offense but because they now know that there is no way to recant the un-constructive criticism, vehement tongue-lashing, or disparaging diatribe that they took such effort to dispense in the first place. Though the abuse does not escalate into a physical altercation, the emotional scars can be far more afflicting, cutting deeper than any bruise or laceration ever could. The voices continue to reverberate in the mind of the one who has been most offended.

So by all means, do say what you need to say, but not without first considering how your words may be received. There are almost always more than two sides. While you cannot parse your every word or predict how one might receive what you say, you can certainly check the sincerity of your intentions. Whether you speak it, hum it, or sing it, lift your voice to do good and not harm; soothe, not insult; transform folks, not put or keep them in their place; restore, not ridicule; bring about justice, not judgment; and affect change, not inflict wrath. Yes, "Lift (Your) Every Voice and Sing," but do mark my words.

Dreaming on Purpose

I realize that I am blessed to have had as much time at home with my children, and to be as hands-on as I have been. Though the decision to be a stay-at-home mother hasn't come without personal and financial sacrifice, I am aware that many do consider it a luxury. I would be remiss, however, if I said I never questioned whether I should be doing more, or whether I made the right decision in doing so. Though as mothers, we fundamentally know that being at home with our children is anything but dull, the repetition of appointments, and all that comes with caring for a home and tending to children can feel routine and meaningless when compared to a an exciting job or career.

From the time that I knew I wanted to have children, I knew that I wanted to be the one to raise them, but I never stopped to actually consider how I would accomplish this while pursuing career ambitions that I grew up thinking were so important. I am sure that being raised by my grandmother during my earlier childhood in the Caribbean was an influencing factor in my decision to be at home with my children. My very own mother did not have the same privilege, should she have wanted it. Understandably, she was more concerned about meeting our most basic needs as the sole provider.

As a mother, I've moved several times across the country, and everywhere I've gone, I've had the pleasure of meeting many other stay-at-home mothers who made the same decision, yet struggled with finding purpose. They are also intelligent, spiritually grounded, and equally ambitious. I now call some of these women my sister-girlfriends. They value our connection as women beyond our obvious roles. They understand the need for spaces in which we can speak freely regarding our need to live purposeful and meaningful lives that aren't relegated to us being wives or mothers alone. I once believed that other mothers didn't want to hear more of the same, but the more time I spent with these women, the more I found quite the opposite to be true. Women do want to talk to and listen to each other, and hear that they are not alone. They want to talk about themselves sometimes, and not just compare notes about "the children".

In my relationships with these women, I've learned that the question of purpose will continue to arise, but the answer will also change over time. In our becoming, we experience seasons that, though they test our mettle, will ultimately give us the clarity that we seek. As we share our stories, we unearth our true gifts and realize that some of the dreams we set out to live long ago, before we had children or families of our own, might have been someone else's dream for us, and not our own. The former successes and careers that we previously felt we sacrificed in order to stay home and raise our children, are no longer suited to the persons that we've now become. In the further development of our womanhood, we become unapologetic for our authenticity, as we re-invent ourselves apart from what has been constructed and projected on us as the ideal.

Though some of our dreams have been deferred, they're certainly not dried up, and for very important reasons. Other dreams stood in conflict with our true heart desires. In my case, success at a corporate career meant compromising my desire to raise my own children. I had to find ways to develop my own voice apart from the roles I had chosen, and in turn, I found that all along, my true passion was writing, even while I chased what was someone else's dream for me.

As we live our most public roles yet, mothers also want to be valued as women with equal vision and desires apart from motherhood. Our credibility comes from a deeper-seated wisdom earned through our total life experience and closer self-examination, not only through the roles we play or careers we may have had. We can take great pride in the knowledge that we're planting seeds for generations to come because of this singular and life yielding decision we've made to be the first line of care for our children and families. Yes, we are aware of the privilege of this decision, but we also see it as purposeful work while we tend to our greatest responsibility yet.

PURPOSEFUL INTENTIONS

Harnessing the Creative Spirit

Canyons of dreams
Incomplete thoughts
Caverns of piercing,
penetrating revelations.
Clear as day, yet dark as night.

—AVRIL SOMERVILLE,
Nightfall

Getting My House in Order

I could not wait to be done with my everyday duties to run home to clean one day. I don't always get that excited about cleaning, but this particular day was different. Some call it domestic bliss, but I'd like to think that it was bigger than that. Growing up, I would always hear my grandmother say "cleanliness is next to godliness", and my interpretation of that, simply put, was that God would not be pleased if I, or my surroundings, weren't kept clean.

I seemed to have missed the greater significance of my grandmother's lesson. Havoc seemed to have taken ahold of my house. There was no denying I would have my work cut out for me upon my return. Sure enough, waiting to greet me was a laundry basket full of dirty clothes, a freshly laundered pile on a dining chair, toys on the floor, and filthy dishes on the countertops. The place was one hot mess! Everything sat right where I left them.

Let me be clear; leaving my home in such disarray is not my usual practice, and this organized chaos was no case of negligence. I decided a while back that if I cleaned every single time a space needed cleaning, it would be all that I would do. For some reason, today was different. I was invoked to clean by a more profound, spiritual contemplation. The song "Get Your House in Order" by Dottie Peoples came to mind, though my impetus to clean was not about religion or about the imminent return of Jesus, yet the first two lines which sang, "Get your house in order, do it today. Get your house in order, do it right away" were haunting and petitioned me to attend to the mess that lie before me with unparalleled urgency.

I think that this urgency had more to do with my conscientious effort to adhere to some life goals that included getting my house in order. By "my house," I'm referring to not just that physical space, but that mental and creative space on which all else is based; that space that allows me to be my best and most authentic self. I've been trying in earnest to make sure that more of my energy and attention is focused on those life goals, and aligned with what I say is truly important. Additionally, I had some quiet confirmations on purpose, and an increasingly unapologetic stance about what I believe is the need to have things in order, and not have life haphazardly manage me.

So, as I wiped down counters and swept the corners, I was more mindful that even these mundane tasks have a much more esoteric meaning. As I stood at the kitchen sink, my hands fully immersed in hot, soapy water, scraping hardened cake batter from my youngest daughter's "kitchen experiment," I was mindful that this act of cleaning is not so much about cleaning, as it was about "cleansing." In that space, I was overcome with an uncanny awareness that I am safe, fed, loved, healthy, kept, and steadily moving to be more aligned with what I call Spirit … God.

This quiet "scrubbing" time was what I needed to reflect on stripping away what was no longer needed. This "cleansing" time just felt right. It was part and parcel of the bigger goal of paring down those meaningless assignments and activities that took up far too much of my precious time.

What I now know is that getting my house in order allowed for life-generating pursuits. Eliminating clutter provides room for internal clarity, which makes discernment less arduous, and lends to a deeper introspection about what needs to be done. Cleansing and getting my house in order also helped me to let go of old misgivings and "things" that were no longer welcome. You see, old things only make it more difficult for us to receive new insights about blessings that await.

So, the next time I hear Dottie Peoples crying out for me to get my house in order, I'll look around my home and do some inventory. Will I have reverted to the disorder that characterized my physical space, or will I hold on to this new orderliness? This is the true challenge of consistency. In the meantime, I hope I don't hear that song any time soon.

Stealing Time

I used to get frustrated about not yet being published or even having a completed draft of a book ready in the event that some angelic literary agent availed himself. More recently, however, I am beginning to understand that life unravels on its own terms despite our best planning. Like waves, the interruptions are ongoing and sure to come, though not at intervals you can ever predict. I'm learning to brace myself for the detours, and "make the time" for writing, listening, and for processing the streams of consciousness that flow during the quiet and sometimes not-so-quiet, though still reflective moments. Sometimes, I "steal" the time in small ways. I resist the urge to respond to every call or suggestion that I participate in yet another school activity, or run that additional errand for the sake of efficiency. I laugh now at my previous preoccupation with "keeping it all together" by having every room cleaned, load washed, or nutritious meal prepared. The tendency to keep everything straight-laced when you don't work outside the home is a real, not perceived one. Though it can be said that I can benefit from more downtime, I find that long periods of it simply do not exist, but rather, time has to be managed.

So now, when I get the urge to watch mindless TV, including the news and silly vices like reality TV, I pass. I convince myself that watching will quickly shrink my brain cells, and choose instead to write something—anything. I tell myself that if there's "breaking news" that is so important, I will learn of it some other way. If I experience writer's block or just can't seem to move the story forward, I'll write something else. I justify that thank-you notes, editorial responses, and letters are all legitimate ways of investing in my writing. Despite a larger story feeling urgent, there isn't always enough time to move it forward. Still, I am attuned to the need for developing at the craft of writing, for putting in the time. I have to trust that Spirit will facilitate its coherence and assembly somewhere down the road.

Also, I find encouragement in many of authors I admire. They too, were once undiscovered and unpublished. Surely, they had a lot to manage in the way of family and work, despite the urgency of their writing. They had to steal the time in many creative and unconventional ways, I imagine, to get the story completed before bringing it to the world. Before becoming well-known, or published authors, many of these authors— mostly women, were once simply women who struggled with managing their passion for writing with the vicissitudes of life; their work did not see the light of day until they were good and grown, much like me! I suppose before then, we haven't lived or experienced enough that qualifies us to speak and share with the world. Probably better said is, unless we have experienced some things, we do not have the wisdom, let alone the voice, for telling a story in a way that a reader would find credible or relevant. I take courage and comfort in that.

Such was the case with the remarkably wise and masterful storyteller J. California Cooper, author of several novels, including some of my favorites, *Some Soul to Keep* and *Family*, and Bebe Moore Campbell, author of *Your Blues Ain't Like Mine* and several more critically acclaimed novels. And although Dr. Maya Angelou traveled worldwide and had done a multiplicity of things in her lifetime, the world did not know of Maya Angelou as a novelist until she published *I Know Why The Caged Bird Sings*. She was already forty-two. I am reminded that venerated artists weren't always such; some of them wrote quietly behind the scenes in the living room and kitchen, crafting stories in their head, on napkins and around their busy lives and children—like Toni Morrison, author of *Song of Solomon* and *God Help the Child*— long before the internet and blogs, and long before they had completed manuscripts fit to print.

Alice Munro was one such woman. Munro is the author of several books including *Dear Life: Stories* and *Lives of Girls and Women: A Novel* and winner of the 2013 Nobel Prize in

Literature for being a "master of the contemporary short story." When asked how consumed she is by the story when she begins to write, she answered "desperately." She later added, "But, you know I always got lunch for my children, did I not? I was a housewife, so I learned to write in times off." Evidently, making the most of the meantime to write something— even if the time afforded comes in snatches at a time—is better than not writing at all.

Being vs. Creating

"Stop trying ... surrender ... learn to just let it be." These words, spoken by Richard from Texas, played by Richard Jenkins, to Groceries, played by Julia Roberts, in *Eat Pray Love*, aren't prophetic, but they are timely as I consider how I tend my time. I'd been struggling with the notion of creating versus being, and it seemed that my "creative" time was being eclipsed by the hurried pace and demands of life.

I'd been taking care of matters of the heart, pressing matters that left unattended would not get done. Some of these included: meal planning for three growing children with discriminating palates; nurturing emotional Ouchy Boo-boos; planning and coordinating all activities, appointments, and everything in between; and finally, being an advocate for my precious children's education, tirelessly and fearlessly challenging head-on persons, procedures, and "principles" that continue to fail our children.

The latter took every nerve and sinew of my being, because the off-handed dismissals by advocates-in-name-only were several, as were the excuses and reasons given for why things are "just the way they are." I am probably no different from other mothers and wives in this regard, but unlike some, I'd become very passionate about creating, writing, and getting in the flow and rhythm of my writing. I imagine that I am also like other writers and artists, who may become anxious when they cannot strike a balance between being and creating. Out of necessity, I've had to negotiate a space between the two. I've had to tend to my time differently, and I'm learning some amazing things in the process.

Each act of love and nurture; each release and touch; and each occasion, is also an important and delicate part of creating. Each moment of being competes to be part of the ultimate story, the creation itself. I see it unfolding and can't quite grasp the intricacies fast enough. However fleeting, I am aware of their fullness, and the indelible mark that they attempt to leave on my heart, in the tapestry that I so desperately want to weave. And as much as I want to sit before that tapestry and tend to it only, and be fully engaged in its coming together, I know that "being" is as necessary as creating, because it is in so being that the epiphanies will come. It's while doing the seemingly mundane, and even the ordinary, that the bursts of creativity enter—while in the car awaiting the green light; waiting for the T-Ball game to end; standing in the checkout line at the grocery store; and even while folding that last load of laundry.

So apart from the need to create, I must also tend time differently in order to respond to matters of the heart, and learn to just be. I'm learning to surrender to the need for that space, all while being attuned to the distinction, as well as the inextricable link between the two. I take comfort that the transformations are still taking place, regardless of where my feet are anchored, or how I'm tending my time at any given moment.

All Vision, All Jobs

I'm sure that I am in great company when I say I've had incredible visions, but have oftentimes been too afraid to share them for fear of them not sounding grand enough, revolutionary enough, or thorough enough; however, acting upon these visions is what ultimately distinguishes us from those who do not. Many of us have gifts and talents so innate in us that we dismiss them as too intuitive, insignificant, small, or common. Our devaluation informs our inaction, keeps us thinking about our futures, while others who've assigned their visions with greater value, move forward. The doers are able to envision their gifts at work and in a larger context beyond their gifts alone. It isn't that they are more equipped or talented, but despite not having all the answers, they are willing to take the risk, and less afraid of being wrong.

The sad news of the passing of Steve Jobs in 2011 made many of us think about our own visions, and whether we are doing sufficient work toward making them a reality. Lucky for us, we got a glimpse into what made Jobs, former CEO and brainchild of Apple Computer, a man more than worth noting. In one commencement address, Jobs emphasized the urgency of doing what you love while you are granted with the life to do it. Few demonstrated such ease when speaking of life's brevity and death's certainty as Jobs did. To some, his plain-spokenness about death may have seemed macabre, but the lessons weren't lost on us.

Death's imminence, Jobs concurred, should provide sufficient motivation for us to live our dreams regardless of what the popular vote or economic tide suggests. His rise as Apple's CEO and a leading world innovator is laudable; however, I think that the most brilliant thing about the illustrious life of Steve Jobs was not his career, as much as it was his vision and the credibility that he assigned to his own creative genius. Ultimately, he built a legacy and empire that required no endorsement from the detractors that underestimated the magnitude of his vision. They saw products; he saw a movement.

Surely, not having sufficient resources was a burning issue for Jobs and co-founder Wozniak during the early years when they were trying to develop the market for what they believed was an incredible product. Still, they never abandoned their vision or unique thinking about technology. Both Wozniak and Jobs were gifted in their own right, but the sum of their gifts and passion was even greater. Together, they were hardly willing to acquiesce to the naysayers and doubters. They knew they were on to something, knew that what they had to offer was ingenious, out-of-the-box, anything but ordinary, and remained absolute in their resolve that folks would eventually catch up.

Jobs and Wozniak firmly believed that their concept was worthy of standing on its own merit, and refused to join the ranks of me-too products that provided only negligible improvements over the products that were already being offered in the PC marketplace. The perception that their products were too niche for a larger mass market did little to dissuade them from moving forward. Now, that's some radical vision right there! One might ask, "How do I get just a little bit of that kind of vision?"

I am a firm believer that we are to maximize life between the bookends of birth and death. Perhaps you are also, but never thought of it quite that way. Life is to be lived with purpose, courage, and a fierce determination about the legacies we wish to create. Many of the answers have to do with how far we can actually see into our future. Do we see books, films, and plays beyond our writing, organizations beyond our activism, schools of empowerment beyond our affirmations? Do we see detail—the final product, the physical structures and dwellings in which our visions are nurtured and brought to life, and the people and players that work to facilitate those visions? Are we radical enough to trust ourselves and plan as though we believe that we can truly accomplish more, beyond

112

the conception of a new idea or thought, or do we get paralyzed when we don't have all the answers? Here's an even bigger question: do we even consider ourselves worthy of the success that would result if we were to follow through with the epiphanies and moments of clarity that we receive? I've heard the question asked of self-help gurus and personal coaches, "What's holding you back?" I think a better question is "Are you courageous enough?" Some call the difference between go-getters and those crippled by fear "moxie"—a special brand of fearless, risk-taking leadership.

The words of Steve Jobs were not new, but the inspiration from someone who'd been clearly walking his own talk, was timely. Until then, the contents of my vision were like bits and pieces of a really good novel, but only loosely stringed together in separate notebooks, strewn on post-its and cocktail napkins. Hearing Steve Jobs, a creative genius by most accounts, speak of the indomitable convictions he had about his own gifts, was tangible evidence of a vision fulfilled. Perhaps my vision wasn't a series of parts after all, but something remarkably beautiful, whole, and very much possible. Jobs's example is proof positive that when you're on to something, and it won't let you go, then it's probably best to just "go with it!"

Why Wait for Perfect?

I am my own worst critic. If I feel like I've missed the mark somehow, I refrain from publicly sharing what I have written. In essence, I have created a standard that has become impossible to uphold as consistently as I'd like, for whatever reason. Lately however, I am finding that waiting for perfect to act, write, move, speak, or simply make a decision is a great disservice to myself and, to a lesser degree, to others.

A perfect example of this happened once when I was invited to speak at an event. I gladly accepted the opportunity and couldn't wait to take my inspiration and energy off the page and on the road! My excitement quickly soured when I learned that I would be sharing the event with another speaker, a published author. I thought, "Damn, I'm not even published yet. With what will I leave our guests?" Honestly, I wrestled with that for a bit, and just then Spirit interrupted.

"You are not there to discuss your writing," it said, "or even that you an aspiring author. You are there to share your own personal journey, your own brand of energy, the convictions of your heart, your Joy, not to be compared to someone else. You were invited and that is enough. You are enough."

This response made me consider the many times that I simply refused to act on something because I didn't have all my ducks lined up in a row, or hesitated to share something laid especially on my heart because it wasn't completely fleshed out. My propensity for perfection and fear of not getting my precise message across caused me to withdraw myself reluctantly from exposure. In a sense, I inoculated myself against what I thought would be rejection or failure. Some might attribute this to not being courageous enough; they might very well be right. Others might find themselves fighting with the same instinct to live up to what seems like a self-imposed, arbitrary standard. Where do you find yourself?

I think that a lack of courage and instinct to live up to our own high standards are inextricably linked. Not having the courage to do something for fear of failure or rejection gets in our way of what we say we want – to ultimately become better or more accomplished somehow. Though choosing the path of least resistance feels safe, this choice hardly keeps us from becoming our most resilient selves. Moreover, showing up only when we feel our best gives others who are also struggling with the same insecurities and fears, the impression that the journey is one of relative ease.

It is important to show up even when we do not have all the answers. In the process, we learn what not to do and amass many lessons that we can then share with others. Though we are certain that nothing is ever perfect, and at times perfectly uncertain, we must allow the Universe to align with us and usher in the right forces and persons that can help take our less-than-stellar life performances from mediocre to masterful. Certainly there's merit in good preparation, but perfection gets far more credit than it deserves.

The Blessing of Invisible Ink

After more than eight decades of living, and well over four of publishing novels—including her most recent *God Help the Child*, and masterpieces such as *Tar Baby*, *Song of Solomon* and *The Bluest Eye*—it is no doubt that Toni Morrison has garnered quite a body of wisdom. So, when I had the blessing to see and hear her lecture on the power of "Invisible Ink," I knew I was in for a real treat.

The depth, soul, and complexity of Morrison's work are matchless and contain works that forge a literary canon almost unto itself. Morrison's isn't complex for the sake of being complex, or to confuse the reader; rather, she is quite purposeful in her intentions as author. Sheer mastery. Literary badass.

No word wasted, no metaphor simplified, no character peripheral. Her novels are genre bending, tradition defying, and transcending. They leave us thoughtful and send us on an inward journey to learn more, both about life and ourselves. The combination of these talents is possessed in the gift that is the one and only, illustrious Toni Morrison.

Once the room finally quieted and everyone had taken their seats, winner of the Presidential Medal of Freedom (2012), Pulitzer Prize for Fiction, (1988, *Beloved*), and The Nobel Prize in Literature (1993), Toni Morrison pronounced her first words. "I'm worth it," she said. She laughed knowingly, owning this declaration. She was not the picture of the imposing or towering Toni Morrison that I had ingrained in my head for years, but one older and less animated, still worth it. From her wheelchair, she scanned the room slowly, looked up to the balcony, and smiled widely and appreciatively at the throngs of people gathered to hear her.

Morrison's delivery was one part patient, two parts assured and unapologetic. She took her time as she leafed through her physical pages, ordering them on the presentation table buttressed against her. The audience fell silent again and waited with bated breath. Morrison's quiet pauses were deliberate and successful in admonishing us to pay close attention as she prepared to impart an important lesson. Her time was not to be wasted. She leaned forward as she began to speak. Older folk used to say, "I'm only going to say this once, so you better listen real well the first time." I didn't want to miss a single word. I leaned in, listening intently, as if we were the only two in the room.

My mouth remained shut, my ears peeled, and my eyes were like lasers—dead set on Morrison's silver locs, pursed mouth, and those contemplative, aged eyes. I was so focused, that at some point, her figure began to blur. She reminded us, and apologized, for not being able to stay afterward to talk or sign autographs. Miss Morrison had taken her respectable and rightful place as an experienced and wise elder as she began to teach those of us who sat in awe of her. She was now one of the "older folk," and I was hungry for anything she was willing to spare. Even a morsel would be plenty.

Morrison described the "Invisible Ink" as that metaphysical place where the right reader connects with the text in a most intimate and personal way, beyond simply finding a book relatable. She elaborated further that not every reader will develop that relationship with the text despite the author's intentions, and that's also okay. The right reader, however, will spot the invisible ink and participate in the story, ultimately helping to write it and fill in the unwritten gaps. When that happens, the text is effective in seducing that reader, bringing him or her into a world beyond the pages.

Her words became fainter as she spoke while the precision and trust of my own voice grew, settling its more pronounced edges around me like a cape, or rather, a royal robe with which Miss Toni Morrison seemed to be gifting me just then, as an ancestor would a family heirloom. I felt spiritually full and emptied all at once, eternally thankful for the abundance of spirit that I've encountered in Morrison's books; her legacy of, and respect for, literary scholarship; and, now in her person.

Even as she was escorted off the stage, and the last round of applause was fading, she seemed to be speaking directly into my spirit.

I took in every inch of her that I could still see—her billowing grey sweater over the arms of her wheelchair; the cascade of silver locs hanging off her back; full, rounded shoulders, turned slightly in, as her hands secured precious papers on her lap—until she was no longer in view. I could hear the words that remained unspoken: "Remember, I've made a way that you might."

Aha! The invisible ink had leapt off the pages, imbuing me with an overwhelming sense of responsibility as a writer, breathing its very life through Morrison's spoken words and spirit, as if it was speaking these words to me:

Remember, I've made a way that you might.
I've *made* a way that you might.
A *way* that you might.
That *you* might.
Indeed, Ms. Morrison was worth it.

How Dare You Say Goodbye?

I sit here grieving you again.

Moments of clarity and rational thought come
But are soon stymied by your unsolicited surprise visits.

Reminders of you abound wherever I go.
The mention of your name,
Reflection on a memory,
Leaves a pit in my chest every single time.

Who are you to figure so prominently in my mind, and
What does your power to do so suggest?

Why have you come back to haunt my thoughts, and
Find new territory in my landscape?

Hours go by and I think not about you … yet
You return, darting in and out of my field of vision
like a child trying to get away with a forbidden act
this one last time.

You skirt the borders of my most empowering moments -
the ones in which I rationalize our breakup, and
perch yourself all poised-like
on the ledges of the windows -
the ones through which I thought
I could envision life without you.

Refusing to let me let you go
Unforgiving and relentless
in your total pursuit of me.

EPILOGUE

I am afraid
Afraid that should I return to you,
you will be no good for me.

Afraid that perhaps
I fell too hard
Loved too big
Grew too joyful
Or worse yet, made myself at home.

Bibliography

Robert Lowry. *Shall We Gather at the River?* 1864. Vinyl recording.

Still Bill. Dir. Prudence Arndt, Damani Baker, John Fine, Alex Vlack, Andrew Zuckerman. Perf. Bill Withers. B-Side Entertainment and Roco Films, 2009. DVD.

Grover Washington, Jr. and Bill Withers. *Winelight.* "Just the Two of Us." Elektra Records, 1980. CD.

"Race 2012: A Conversation About Race and Politics in America." *PBS.org. 2012 Race Blogging Project.* Web. 3 Oct. 2012. <http://race2012pbs.org/election/blog-page/>

"Significant Doubts About Troy Davis' Guilt: A Case for Clemency." *NAACP.org.* Web. 14 May 2015. <http://www.naacp.org/pages/troy-davis-a-case-for-clemency/ >

"Trayvon Martin Shooting: Fast Facts." *CNN.com.* Web. 14 May 2015. <http://www.cnn.com/2013/06/05/us/trayvon-martin-shooting-fast-facts/ >

The Wiz. Dir. Sidney Lumet. Perf. Diana Ross, Michael Jackson, Nipsey Russell. Universal Studios Home Entertainment, 2010. DVD.

Baum, Frank L. *The Wonderful Wizard of Oz.* Chicago: George M. Hill Company, 1900. Print.

BIBLIOGRAPHY

Obama, Barack. "Celebrating Father's Day." White House. Washington, D.C. 18 June 2011. Weekly Address.

Johnson, James Weldon. "Lift Every Voice and Sing." *Selected American and British Poems*. Lit2Go Edition. 1900. Web. May 13, 2015. <http://etc.usf.edu/lit2go/109/selected-american-and-british-poems/5239/lift-every-voice-and-sing/>

Dottie Peoples and The People's Choice Chorale. *On Time God*. "Get Your House in Order." Atlanta International Records, Inc., 1994. CD.

"Alice Munro - Nobel Lecture." *Nobelprize.org*. Nobel Media AB 2014. Web. 13 May 2015. <http://www.nobelprize.org/nobel_prizes/literature/laureates/2013/munro-lecture_en.html/>

Jobs, Steve. "You've Got to Find What You Love." Stanford University. Stanford, CA. 12 June 2005. Commencement Address.

Morrison, Toni. "Invisible Ink." Swarthmore College. Swarthmore, PA. 7 April 2014. Lecture and Reading.

About the Author

Writer, essayist, and poet AVRIL SOMERVILLE is also the author of the upcoming, highly anticipated novel, *How Dare You Say Goodbye?* In May 2015, her poem, "Massive Cover-Up," was selected for performance at the Art Sanctuary of Philadelphia's 31st Annual Celebration of Black Writing Festival, an event renowned for featuring some of the region's most talented authors and artists. For information on Avril Somerville's speaking and author engagements, please visit www.somerempress.com.